Steamboat

Ski Town USA

by Tom Bie

TO MIKE & BARBARA—
   COME OUT TO STEAMBOAT MORE
OFTEN! (AND KEEP ENJOYING THOSE CLOUDS.)

Tom Bie
JAN 2003

MOUNTAIN SPORTS PRESS

BOULDER, COLORADO USA

Steamboat: Ski Town USA.

Published by Mountain Sports Press

Distributed to the book trade by:
PUBLISHERS GROUP WEST

Bill Grout, *Editor-in-Chief*
Michelle Klammer Schrantz, *Art Director*
Alan Stark, *Associate Publisher*
Scott Kronberg, *Associate Art Director*
Chris Salt, *Production Manager*
Andy Hawk, *Sales Representative*
Megan Selkey, *Designer*
Tom Bie, *Photo Editor*

Champagne Powder® is a registered trademark of the Steamboat
Ski & Resort Corporation.

Ski Town USA® is a registered trademark of the Steamboat Springs
Winter Sports Club.

ISBN 0-9717748-4-6
Library of Congress Cataloging-in-Publication Data applied for.

Printed in Canada by Friesens Corporation

Prepress by Westphal West, Boulder, Colorado

A subsidiary of:

929 Pearl Street, Suite 200
Boulder, CO 80302
303-448-7617

To my parents, Jean and LeRoy Bie,

for their undying support of my questionable

career choices in mountain towns.

contents

Preface By Billy Kidd

Growing up as a young ski racer in Stowe, Vermont, I'd heard of Steamboat Springs, Colorado. This was partially because America's best skier at the time, Buddy Werner, was a hero of mine, and he was from Steamboat, and also because so many Olympic skiers came from Steamboat. My dad had been skiing out West in the 1950s, he told me how great the skiing was in the Rockies, and I heard that the people in Colorado were friendly and the snow was light and plentiful. So Steamboat was on my mind long before I moved here.

But it wasn't until I came to town in 1970, when I was invited to be the resort's Director of Skiing, that I began to appreciate exactly how special this town and mountain are. I felt comfortable here right away, because it looked and felt much like Vermont. Both Stowe and Steamboat are ski towns, and Vermont's dairy farming seemed similar to cattle ranching in Colorado. In both places the people make guests feel welcome, but in Steamboat I could wear a cowboy hat and pretend I'm a real cowboy.

For Eastern kids growing up in America in the 1950s—especially for boys—fantasizing about being Roy Rogers or The Lone Ranger, the West was a magical, mythical place. Every kid had a cowboy-theme lunchbox, bronco pajamas, or a felt cowboy hat. So coming to the town of Steamboat Springs, where everything about the landscape and the atmosphere and the people was authentic and Western, was a dream come true for me.

I've never gotten over how genuinely warm Steamboat's residents are. I recall a visitor asking me, "I can understand how you can train 400 employees on the mountain to be friendly and courteous, but how do you train the lady at the grocery store checkout counter? Or the kid pumping gas?" I told him that's just how people are in Steamboat.

The resort itself was dreamed up, planned and developed by local ranchers, men such as Jim Temple and John Fetcher, who worked with their hands to create a great ski hill. And though Steamboat remains a small town, its residents are worldly because so many of them have traveled the globe as competitive skiers, and because our guests come from around the world. Which is no surprise to me, since I think that the best skiing in the world is right here in the Rocky Mountains!

Living in Steamboat, I've continued my connection to the Olympics. When you're here, you can see why the place has produced so many Olympians. Locals take enormous pride in volunteering and participating in events—whether it's a grade school ski race, the Special Olympics World Winter Games, the annual Cowboy Downhill, or a World Cup competition. Even ranchers who don't ski will be out on the slopes volunteering and cheering on the competitors.

I have felt lucky to have an association with Steamboat for 33 years. Steamboat Ski Resort and Ski Town USA will surely continue to lead the way in producing future Olympians, great vacations and my favorite...Champagne Powder snow.

Billy Kidd, 1964 Olympic medalist and 1970 World Champion, has been Director of Skiing at Steamboat Ski Resort since 1970.

Introduction

"Kiss the mountain air we breathe."
—Widespread Panic

Get up early, at least once, on a powder day. Because when the snow falls hard and heavy in a ski town, the true character of the community emerges, and nowhere is this more true than in Steamboat Springs, Colorado.

Certainly there are bigger mountains, places where the slopes are steeper or the runs longer or the views more majestic. But nowhere do the various parts add up to create such an exceptional mix. A powder day comes to Steamboat like the perfect meal, paradise presented on a silver platter. To get off the lift at the top of Storm Peak and push off into a foot of fresh is to immerse yourself in precisely what remains—and will always remain—so great about the sport of skiing.

At the top of Mount Werner, you can fall in love with the color of light almost any time of day, whether you're weaving through aspens on a frozen February morning or gazing down at the valley during an autumn afternoon, sweat dripping onto your mountain bike tire. It's a ski hill that welcomes all comers—families, fanatics, freaks, powderhounds and purists, bump lovers and beginners still searching for that first hockey stop. Steamboat invites more than it intimidates, giving those who ski here less a sense of dominance than of belonging.

Through nearly a decade of writing for *Skiing* and *Powder* magazines, I've been lucky to visit many ski areas in the country. And I can say with certainty that Steamboat and its people represent the best of what we all love about mountain towns in America. To many people, skiing is a sometimes cold pastime that fills a couple of weekends a year because it's less boring than lawn darts and cheaper than golf. But not here. Here you have the vision of a Jim Temple, the dedication of a Gordy Wren, the persistence of a John Fetcher, the heart of a Buddy Werner, the passion of a Carl Howelsen and the encouragement of a town willing to embrace a sport so strongly that its native sons and daughters will dedicate a lifetime to perfecting it.

Steamboat has long been known as "Ski Town USA" and the home of "champagne powder," but beyond the catchy marketing phrases is a much deeper, more intimate connection to the sport. This town is famous for its Olympians, for its storied competitors of a bygone era, for its great snowfalls of '83 and '96. There's so much history that you often forget the best ski days may be yet to come. Your best Steamboat ski day ever may begin tomorrow morning.

I lived in Steamboat only two short years—long enough to learn some, but not all, of the stories in this book. The rest came from more than 50 hours of interviews I conducted with some of the people who made this town what it is today. I enjoyed the interviews immensely, and I hope you enjoy the result.

Tom Bie
Boulder, Colorado
November 2002

Chapter 1

The Pioneers

Hahns Peak, where German prospector Joseph Hahn discovered gold in 1865, drawing hundreds of settlers to Northwest Colorado.

James Harvey Crawford didn't know he was founding a ski town when he became Steamboat's first homesteader in June of 1874. It just worked out that way. Only a few years earlier, Crawford had been living in relative comfort on a farm south of Sedalia, Missouri, with his wife, Maggie, and three young children. But a train trip to Denver with his brother and brother-in-law in the summer of 1872 left the Missouri farmer with an image of mountains that he couldn't shake. Besides, like many residents of today's mountain towns, Crawford had what his wife referred to as a "roving disposition," and the pull of the Rockies was as strong in the 1800s as it is today.

By the following spring, Crawford had convinced Maggie that heading west would be a good idea—or at least an adventurous one. So he sold his farm, and the family struck out on May 1, 1873, with a train of seven wagons, and spent 35 days making their way to Denver. But that wasn't far enough west to satisfy Crawford. He wanted to see the *other* side of the Rockies, the "wondrous" country of

James Harvey Crawford (1845–1930), Steamboat's first settler.

Though the number of ranches is decreasing, raising cattle—and hay—remains a Western way of life in the Yampa Valley, just as it was in the early 1900s.

tall timber and lush valleys he'd read about in an article in the *Missouri Republican*.

So Crawford embarked on a string of scouting expeditions through the countryside beyond the Continental Divide, and during one such trip he ran into a wandering gold prospector working his way south toward Breckenridge. The man told Crawford about a beautiful valley with bubbling hot springs where the Bear River (what the Yampa was then called) made a big bend to the west.

Crawford and a few scouting companions set out for "the big bend." When he reached the hot springs the prospector had mentioned, Crawford decided he'd found paradise, declaring, "This is the place for me." So the young Civil War veteran picked out his spread near the river and posted his homestead claim on a nearby tree. The group then returned to Hot Sulphur Springs, where he had built a temporary home for his family. But Crawford worried all the next winter that somebody might head up to Steamboat

Maggie Crawford, wife of James Crawford, and founder of Steamboat's first church, school and library.

and jump his claim. So early the following spring, he and a man named Lute Carlton set out to return to the Yampa Valley and ensure the safety of his land.

It took them three weeks to travel from Hot Sulphur Springs to Steamboat, a trip that now takes a little over an hour. They were on skis most of the way, pulling a sled through the deep snows of the Gore Range. Upon reaching the Yampa, the two discovered that nobody had tampered with Crawford's claim, so after a few days of improvements to what would become Steamboat's first home, the pair returned to Hot Sulphur Springs. Crawford made the 90-mile odyssey back to Steamboat one more time later that summer, bringing his family along with him—John and Logan, four and five, respectively, and older sister Lulie, who was seven. (All of these early trips from Hot Sulphur Springs to Steamboat entered the Yampa Valley from the south, over Lynx Pass, passing just east of where the town of Oak Creek now sits. Nobody tackled the shorter but considerably higher Rabbit Ears Pass for another 30 years.)

Like many who followed after him, Crawford was drawn to the Yampa Valley by what he'd heard and read about the area: that it was beautiful, that it offered opportunity, that it might be a good place to raise a family. But he was also pulled by a decade of dreaming about staking his own claim. After 70 years of heated debate over the distribution of public lands, the Homestead Act had become law in 1862, and James Harvey Crawford used it on June 24, 1874, to become the first settler in the verdant mountain valley of Steamboat Springs. As hard as it is to fathom in the contemporary world of Western land values, the Homestead Act allowed any U.S. citizen to claim 160 acres of public land as his own. And, as long as certain criteria were met—such as building a house, putting up some fencing and actually living there for a period of five years—the land belonged to the person who settled it. (If you're thinking about driving out to stake your claim, don't bother. In 1976, the Homestead Act expired in every state but Alaska, where it ended 10 years later.)

Crawford didn't come up with the town name—that was

James Crawford (on wagon), with a few of his fellow pioneers. Crawford built his one-room cabin near what is now Iron Spring Park, at the west end of town. It later served as both the first post office (1878) and the first school (1883).

bestowed by some of the valley's earlier visitors, trappers who heard the *chug-chug* of the hot springs flowing into the Yampa River on the west end of town and thought it sounded like a steamboat heading upriver. But Crawford did have a great influence on the community, serving not only as its first mayor but also as its first county judge and superintendent of schools. He also served two terms as a state legislator.

"Crawford was actually the first real estate entrepreneur in the valley," said Jean Wren, a local historian and wife of legendary Steamboat skier Gordy Wren. "He divided and subdivided, and that was the beginning of a long tradition in Routt County."

Maggie Crawford had her own influence on Steamboat, starting the first school, first church and first library, among other things. She also warmed many a cold day for the traveling miner or trapper, offering up the Crawford house as a place for food and shelter. By the time they were teenagers, the Crawford boys, John and Logan, had

"Crawford was actually the first real estate entrepreneur in the valley. He divided and subdivided, and that was the beginning of a long tradition in Routt County."

Perry-Mansfield

The Perry-Mansfield Performing Arts Center, located in scenic and historic Strawberry Park, has played a crucial role in the creative life of Steamboat for almost 100 years. Founded by Charlotte Perry and Portia Mansfield in 1913, the school has become one of the most beloved performing arts camps in the country, introducing dozens of students every summer to the joy of learning dance and theater in the mountains.

Charlotte Perry's family owned an Oak Creek coal mine, and it was Charlotte's sister, Marjorie, who is credited with persuading ski jumper Carl Howelsen to make his now-famous move to Steamboat in 1913. The sisters' father, Samuel Perry, also played an early role in the valley, traveling to England in order to help obtain financing for construction of the Moffat Tunnel for what, at the time, was the highest railroad in North America.

But it was Charlotte, an actress, who dared open an arts school during a time when the words "dancing girls" meant something else entirely. The first camp had 12 students, but plenty of folks in town didn't much care for the idea of two women teaching young girls anything in the wilderness. The issue was made even more sensitive by the existence of a brothel that operated at that time in Brooklyn, a section of town across the Yampa River. But opinions changed as soon as local girls began attending Perry-Mansfield. In a 1917 article following an early public performance, the *Steamboat Pilot* had this to say: "The first season of the school three years ago created somewhat of a sensation because many of the dances were characteristically given in bare feet, but the early critics subsided after seeing a performance and realizing that nothing was sought nor attained except enhancement of grace and beauty of the movements. The school gradually has gained favor until now it attracts students from the leading families of the United States."

Throughout the 1960s, various aspects of the Perry-Mansfield school were slowly sold off to Stephens College, in Columbia, Missouri. But the Friends of Perry-Mansfield—a local group led by Holly Williams—bought the arts center back in September 1993 for $1.1 million. "That's just typical of this community," says local historian and former Steamboat High School librarian Jayne Hill, of the group that bought back Perry-Mansfield. "People here take great pride in carrying on history and tradition—and the Perry-Mansfield school is part of that."

The original 15-acre Perry–Mansfield campus has now grown to almost 100 acres, and is sprinkled with aspens, conifers and rustic cabins. The school has helped produce many fine actors and actresses—including Julie Harris and Dustin Hoffman—and continues its long tradition of instruction in equestrian disciplines. In addition to offering coed residential and day classes, various public performances of music, theater and dance take place throughout July and August.

Top: Portia Mansfield herself choreographed the early dance performances.
Bottom: Jinney Mansfield, Portia's cousin (on left). Before Jinney's father left for the Navy, his parting advice was "Don't go to dance camp." She later became a professional.

A group of campers—including a young Dustin Hoffman (lower right)—enjoys a story by Barney Brown, Hollywood coach for the Perry-Mansfield drama department.

found their own source of income in the area: guiding big game hunts for wealthy Eastern clients.

Colorado was not necessarily a safe haven for whites in the 1870s, however. Many Indians in the area were still angry over the Sand Creek Massacre of November 1864, in which U.S. troops attacked a tribe of Cheyenne and Arapaho camping in Southeastern Colorado, killing more than 100—many of them women and children.

Even closer to home was the Meeker Massacre: In 1879, Utes killed Indian agent Nathan Meeker and 10 other men west of Steamboat. Despite this and other tensions in the region, relations between the Crawfords and several of the valley's Ute families were reportedly cordial. Chief Colorow had visited the Crawfords in both Hot Sulphur Springs and Steamboat, though it was often to ask for food. Colorow is frequently mentioned as one of the most powerful and influential Ute Chiefs of the time. But ironically, Colorow wasn't a Ute: He'd been stolen from Comanches as a small

child. In 1881, the Utes—the oldest continuous residents of Colorado—were forcibly removed to the Uinta Indian reservation in Utah.

As remote as the Yampa Valley must have seemed when the Crawfords arrived, it wasn't completely isolated. Just 30 miles north, a German immigrant named Joseph Hahn had discovered gold in 1865, causing many who'd been through the valley before Crawford to bypass Steamboat in favor of Hahns Peak, where more than 2,000 people were living by the mid 1870s.

"It was an important place," said Wren, of Hahns Peak in the early days. "It was lively and large, because it was a mining center." Hahns Peak was also Routt county's seat, from the creation of the county in 1879 until 1912. There was plenty of controversy when it was moved to Steamboat. "There was a big fight over that," Wren said. "The business owners, especially, thought the county seat should stay up there."

Routt County was named after John L. Routt, the

Opposite page: On the road to Hahns Peak, late 1920s.
Below: Chief Colorow was friendly with the early Steamboat settlers.

Below top: Children at Hahns Peak, in their Sunday best.
Below bottom: Skiers in skirts were a common sight before World War I.

Anyone who has ever driven to Steamboat has seen the famous F.M. Light & Sons road signs, which start appearing just west of Kremmling or east of Maybell or south of the Wyoming border. They advertise cowboy hats and denim wear and a friendly atmosphere with a fair price. No visitor can miss them, and that's precisely the point. They've been standing in those Colorado fields since three Light brothers—Day, Clarence (C.W.) and Olin—started putting them up in 1928. And they won't be coming down anytime soon.

Francis Marion Light, the schoolteacher from Ohio who arrived in Steamboat with his wife, seven kids and a dog, knew a bargain when he saw one. Even in 1905, $1,000 seemed a fair price for a chunk of land along Lincoln Avenue. So Francis Light—better known as Frank—bought the lot from town founder James Crawford, and the retail world in Steamboat was forever altered.

During the mid 1920s, the Great Depression was taking its toll on every business in America, and F.M. Light & Sons was no exception. But Frank's sons Day and C.W. decided they weren't going to just sit idly by. The brothers bought a couple of modified panel trucks, then headed out to area ranches in search of orders they weren't getting in town. And they found them. Customers bought cowboy boots, cowboy hats and other clothing. They bought saddles for their horses and got news from town in the process. Three of F.M. Light's sons had figured out a way to ease the pain of the Depression, and their "store on

Top: One of dozens of F.M. Light & Sons signs scattered about the Northwestern Colorado landscape.
Bottom: Clarence Light, standing beside the company's early "store on wheels," 1928.

wheels" service grew to include western Wyoming and all of Colorado operating into the 1970s. Another wise business move in the 1920s occurred when F.M. Light & Sons became the first place in town to sell ski clothes, as well as Groswold skis, which were made in Denver.

One classic story from 1914 tells about the time that Olin and C.W. took their six-shooters and chased down a customer who'd given them a bad check. The guy had bought around $2 in merchandise and presented an $8 check, which Olin cashed for him. After going to the bank and discovering that the check was no good, the brothers grabbed their guns and found the thief walking across town on his way to the gambling houses and saloons in Brooklyn, the red-light district on the south side of the river. The two cornered the crook and got their money and merchandise back.

Yet the famous yellow signs remain the trademark of the family store. Their appropriateness has been debated over for years and their effectiveness has been the subject of lectures by college marketing professors. "We used to have over 300," says Lloyd Lockhart, who owned the store with his wife, Annabeth—C.W. Light's daughter—from 1964 to 1967. "Now I think it's around 100 or so. It's always surprising whenever we hire new help in the store—they just can't believe how many people come in the front door just to say they saw the signs and wanted to stop. You hear it a hundred times a day." ✐

Francis Marion ("F.M.") Light and Stardust.

governor at the time, who designated Hahns Peak as the temporary county seat. The towns of Hayden and Craig also wanted to be county headquarters, but squabbles between them meant that neither could ever get the required votes to make it happen. Finally, in 1911, the state legislature split Routt into two separate counties, creating Moffat County from the part of Routt that included Craig and, thereby, removing Craig from the running. In the general election in November, Steamboat easily won out over Oak Creek and has remained the county seat ever since.

Almost 90 years would pass between Crawford's arrival and the first steps toward what would eventually become Steamboat Ski Resort. But the sport itself was well established by the early 1900s. Mail carriers and doctors had been using skis for several years.

"What the mail carriers used, you *could* call skis," said Wren, whose uncle George was one of the first mail carriers in the valley. "But I wouldn't call what they did skiing. They used big jumping skis that wouldn't turn, and they sat on a stick

and used it as a rudder. You'd just lean to one side or the other to steer, and if you wanted to slow down you just sat on it."

But not all skiing at Hahns Peak was for work. "Skiing and sled riding were indulged nearly every night," wrote C.A. Morning, who served as county judge from 1905 to 1925. Also, early issues of the *Routt County Sentinel*, the valley's first newspaper, mention various winter sports taking place at Hahns Peak in the early 1900s. And Thelma Stevenson's book, *Historic Hahns Peak*, describes "flying bird" ski jumping contests organized along the Encampment River as early as 1905.

Others soon joined the Crawfords in Steamboat, and the town grew from about five families to 100 in less than 20 years. By the time it was incorporated at the turn of the century, the population was 595. Shops started appearing on Lincoln Avenue, places like J.W. Hugus & Co., F.M. Light & Sons, and Steamboat Mercantile, where Northland skis were sold. Steamboat Mercantile was originally located up at Hahns Peak, where it was called Wither's Mercantile. Archie Wither and his three brothers had opened it there

Opposite page: The Crawford boys, John and Logan, enjoy a few turn-of-the-century turns. The two would later become the first hunting guides in the area. Below: An early funeral at Hahns Peak. The men had to put on their skis as soon as they dragged the casket a little farther into the deep snow.

during the gold rush years, and in 1903 the brothers moved it down to Steamboat. Archie and Pearl Wither lived on Wither Hill in the middle of Steamboat, and the Wither name has survived in town for many years. Pete Wither, grandson of Archie, spent 30 years working for the Steamboat Ski Area, including 16 as its ski patrol director.

Many of Steamboat's first visitors came for the healing properties—real or imagined—of the area's many sulfur springs. The Bathhouse Springs, where the Steamboat Health and Recreation Center now sits, was the town's first tourist attraction, drawing everyone from Hahns Peak miners to ailing Easterners looking to cure whatever troubled them.

It may have taken Steamboat even longer to become an incorporated town were it not for a man named G.H. Smedley, who wanted to supply the valley with power. Just before the turn of the century, Smedley rolled in on a stagecoach that shuttled between Wolcott (just west of present-day Vail) to Steamboat. He said he'd be happy to build a

The Bitter Springs, which produced the chugging steamboat sound that gave the town its name. The springs are located across from what is now the Bud Werner library.

power plant if local leaders would be kind enough to incorporate the community. So, led by Crawford himself, that's just what happened in the summer of 1900, and Smedley built his plant later that year right in the center of the new incorporated town of Steamboat. Shortly thereafter, the young city council got to work passing important new laws. Two of the more crucial pieces of legislation made it "unlawful to let one's cow wander in town" or to "have bucking horse contests on Main Street."

Hundreds of stories exist concerning those early, sketchy Wolcott-to-Steamboat stagecoach rides, including many accounts of the coach tipping over or getting stuck in the snow or mud. (Anyone who has driven Colorado 131 during a winter

Opposite page: Over 200 families were living in Steamboat by 1910. Below: Skimming across Bathhouse Springs, Steamboat's first tourist attraction.

Many of Steamboat's first visitors came for the healing properties— real or imagined— of the area's many sulfur springs.

The Shady Side of the River

By Jean Wren

The story of old-time Brooklyn, being a chronicle of brief pleasures, was never properly recorded. After 90 years, the very few who might remember, much wiser now, prefer to forget. The few stories that are still told about Ollie, Gus, Hazel, Shorty, Antone and the rest of the "saloon bunch" stand out like patches of light and color in a darkened room. They were the strangers across the Yampa and the days of their prosperity and decline were recorded only in private memory and the daily accounting of lawmen.

A lively situation had been created, balancing two or three generations of good wives and mothers against a steady invasion of thirsty cowhands. Steamboat Springs had been an upright, God-fearing community from the beginning, with an anti-liquor clause written into each property deed. It was also a booming cow town, in time a railhead, shipping more than 60 cars of livestock each week, in season. It is hard to guess what sort of siege might have developed if the moral climate hadn't eased a bit outside the town limits, across the Second Street bridge. The new community meant booze at 15 cents a shot, women at two dollars a visit, poker, bright lights and nickelodeons, a prospect just short of heaven for men who had been riding herd. It also meant that the ladies on the Godly side of the river could have teas and recitals and sing Christian Temperance hymns in relative peace.

The first kegs had come bouncing over the passes in freight wagons when the town was about 10 years old. By 1890 there were five saloons lined along a dusty track paralleling the south bank of the Yampa. There were also "rooming houses" and "hotels" filled with women with very rosy cheeks. This community of 40 or more regulars had become Brooklyn, named, according to local writer and historian, John Burroughs, by a "consumptive individual who possessed a sense of humor and a flair for liquor, women, and oil paints, in that order, and who hailed from Manhattan Island."

Butch Cassidy and the Wild Bunch were said to have met in Brooklyn after the outbreak of the Spanish-American War, in 1898, to decide if they should volunteer to fight. There were serious misgivings, we are told, most of the Bunch having a heavy notion that they would end up in jail when they were no longer useful to the cause. Patriotism lost out to free enterprise, and there is no record that they visited again.

Antone Kline, owner of the Capital Saloon, was hands-down the most respectable member of the village. A family man, he would allow no women or youngsters on his premises, and his poker tables were honest. He had been a member of the Canadian Northwest Mounted Police for 25 years, and his best friend was Routt County Sheriff Charley Neiman. Antone's son remembered the time a big Swede from a railroad crew stayed after saloon hours to hold up his father.

Antone, polishing glasses behind the bar, pointed to the safe. "It's unlocked," he said. The man opened the safe door and took out a bag of money. "The swinging door at the back is still open," Antone said. The man went back to the door and, in pushing through, half turned. That's when Antone shot him with the .45 he kept under the bar. The

THE OLD BRIDGE

The old bridge to Brooklyn crossed the Yampa near what is now the Fifth Street Bridge.

hand that held the money bag was shattered. The foot dropped to the floor and the saloon man picked up his polishing rag. "Now get the hell out of here," he bellowed.

Eventually, in response to a rising popular sentiment, legislation was passed to make Colorado a dry state, beginning on January 1, 1916. Tall, dark-haired Gus Durbin, a durable Irishman who had kept his saloon open in Brooklyn in spite of unpleasantness with the law, shrugged his shoulders and had a sign painted to put up at the back of the bar: THE FIRST OF JANUARY WILL BE THE LAST OF AUGUST.

Gus had known when to throw his hand in, but there were those who refused to believe the game was over. Lawmen searching Brooklyn on a mid January Sunday in 1916 to make sure the new dry laws were being obeyed found a large cache of alcohol in the Brooklyn home and cellar of A.J. Dixon, the man who had bought out the Capital Saloon. "I have the whole state and the United States behind me," the sheriff proclaimed. "The law is going to be enforced if it takes the entire force of the sheriff's office to do it."

When the "entire force" of the sheriff's office came on duty Monday and went over to Dixon's to make the seizure, they discovered that one large keg of whiskey, full on Sunday, was almost empty. It is downright pleasant to think that Brooklyn went down, all flags flying, with a great big party. &

Jean Wren passed away in the spring of 2002, after becoming one of Steamboat's finest and most respected historians. She was the author of Steamboat Springs and the Treacherous and Speedy Skee, *published in 1972. A longer version of this article first appeared in* Steamboat Magazine *in 1984.*

Booze and Broncs: When "bucking horse contests" were outlawed on Steamboat's Main Street, they were sometimes moved across the river to Brooklyn, near where the rodeo grounds are located today. Shown here is Pershing, a famous bucking bronc from the early 1900s.

storm knows that even now, over 100 years later, the route remains a dicey proposition.) Perhaps no tale better exemplifies the horror of that journey than this excerpt from longtime Steamboat local John Rolfe Burroughs' 1963 book, *Headfirst in the Pickle Barrel*, about growing up in the Yampa Valley:

"It had sleeted the night before, and, descending to the Grand [Colorado] River at State Bridge the first morning out of Wolcott, the road down that steep northern slope was a glaze of ice. At the top of the hill, the driver suddenly snatched the whip out of its socket and lashed the horses into a run, nearly scaring the passengers out of their wits. The hill fell off sharply to water's edge, the road funneling directly onto a narrow wooden bridge over the Grand, which foamed bank-full with spring runoff. The slightest miscalculation on the part of the driver would have meant disaster, but there was no miscalculation. The horses raced down the hill and thundered out onto the bridge, the high-wheeled coach careening behind them."

The evolution of transportation to Steamboat goes something like this: Before 1888, you had to be really good on skis or snowshoes. From 1888 to 1909, people would take the Rio Grande Railroad from Denver to Wolcott—about 80 miles from Steamboat—and then take the Wolcott-to-Steamboat-to-Hahns Peak stagecoach. This was a two-day trip, with an overnight in Yampa.

Then passenger train service came to Steamboat. The Moffat Railroad (also known as the Denver & Salt Lake Railroad) first carried passengers into town during the winter of 1909—ironically, the same year a fire destroyed the stagecoach livery stables. Construction had begun six years earlier, in April 1903. Denver banker David Moffat, looking to strike it rich hauling coal, wanted to build a railroad from Denver all the way to Salt Lake City. He had big plans to blast a two-mile-long tunnel through the Continental Divide, but he ran out of money before he could get the job done. Much of Moffat's borrowed cash went to keeping the 23 miles of track over Rollins Pass—the temporary route the train

Opposite page: From 1888 to 1909 a stagecoach line offered a two-day trip from Wolcott to Steamboat to Hahns Peak.
Below: The Denver & Salt Lake Railroad, 1917. Also called the Moffat Railroad, it brought the first passengers to Steamboat in 1909.

Steamboat, circa 1923. The courthouse (upper left), built the same year, is still standing today.

used while work continued on the tunnel—free of snow during the winter. Steamboat rancher Vernon Summer remembers the trouble the train would have getting over the Divide.

"Because of the terrain, it was always pretty slow getting in here," Summer says. "They had snowsheds over the rails

> With the arrival of train passengers, the people of Steamboat naturally wanted to build a world-class hotel for them to stay in. And that they did, constructing the posh Cabin Hotel.

to try and keep them open, but I can remember that railroad would be blocked for days at a time, and then one day you'd get a whole big pile of mail all at once."

Though Moffat passed away before he finished his hole to the other side of the Divide, a 6.2-mile tunnel through the mountain was finally completed in 1928 and named for the early visionary. The Moffat Tunnel, which today carries passengers from Denver to Winter Park and beyond, cost $18 million and 19 lives. It is the second longest railroad tunnel in the United States.

With the arrival of train passengers, the people of Steamboat naturally wanted to build a world-class hotel for them to stay in. And that they did, constructing the posh Cabin Hotel, featuring 100 guestrooms, a large dining room, and walls decorated with elk and deer heads. The hotel was located at the west end of town, where the Bud Werner Library now sits, making it a convenient walk for guests arriving at the train depot just across the river. The Cabin Hotel burned to the ground in 1939, becoming a pile of ashes in less than 30 minutes. Summer remembers the feelings of at least one disappointed resident. "This one old timer said, 'I waited 30 years to see that thing burn down and then darned if I didn't miss it.'"

The first road over Rabbit Ears Pass was completed in 1914, but that didn't make life much easier for settlers. The potato was a successful crop until the topsoil went bad, and cattle produced good income for a few residents. (For several years, Steamboat's train depot shipped more cattle than any other town in the country). Still, ranching and farming were tough businesses. One of the early and surprising success stories came from an unlikely source: strawberries. Nobody seems to know exactly how the first crop was planted, but a farmer named Lester Remington— who lived near the base of Buffalo Pass, in an area north of town known ever since as Strawberry Park—walked out into his hayfield one day to find several rows of strawberries growing. Because Steamboat was at a higher elevation than most strawberry fields across the country, farmers like

Remington could produce berries later in the season, in August and September—and command premium prices as far away as Chicago. The ensuing booming berry business paid off handsomely, providing Remington and others with a healthy and uncommon source of income for several years, until two years of early frost ended the berry boom.

Strawberry Park was also home to two of Steamboat's most creative and colorful personalities—sisters Charlotte and Marjorie Perry. Both of them spent summers in Steamboat, but Marjorie was one of the first women in the valley to fall in love with skiing. She often stayed through the winter, traveling east to Hot Sulphur Springs for ski meets and other activities. On one such occasion she met a young Norwegian named Carl Howelsen and suggested to him that he should move to Steamboat and organize a winter carnival there. Young Miss Perry must have been persuasive, because Howelsen made the move the following fall, and the town of Steamboat was never the same. ✳

Top: The first road over Rabbit Ears Pass was completed in 1914.
Bottom: Picking berries in Strawberry Park.

Marjorie Perry, about 1967. In her younger days, she fell in love with skiing and talked Carl Howelsen into coming to Steamboat.

Chapter 2

Howelsen Hill

And a Sport Called Ski Jumping

Sky high over Steamboat. Nordic Combined World Cup, 1997.

If you drive through Steamboat early on a winter morning and look south from Lincoln Avenue, past the mist rising from the Yampa River, you will often see skiers on Howelsen Hill—Steamboat's other, lesser known ski resort. But the skiers who draw your attention won't be banging gates or practicing their mogul runs—they'll be flying, literally, toward town and into the record books that have been rewritten dozens of times in almost 90 years of Steamboat jumping history.

To someone unfamiliar with it, Howelsen may appear so small as to be insignificant. But it was here that skiing was largely introduced not just to Steamboat but to Colorado. Only a couple of runs are visible from town, curving down from its east shoulder, with slalom patterns carved into the snow by the town's many junior racers. The ski jumps are obvious, peeking out from the trees just as they've done since Norwegian Carl Howelsen (see sidebar, page 64) built the first one there in 1915.

Howelsen had organized the first Steamboat Springs Winter Carnival the year before, and nothing amazed and inspired the spectators like the jumping events. Just as he

Carl Howelsen, on the cover of the program for the Second Annual Carnival of the Hot Sulphur Springs Winter Sports Club.

Second Annual Carnival
OF THE
Winter Sports Club
OF
HOT SULPHUR SPRINGS. COLO.
January 31st and
February 1st and 2nd, 1913

SKI JUMP

Ragnar Omtvedt's first world championship jump, at Howelsen Hill, Valentine's Day, 1915.

had thrilled those in Chicago and Hot Sulphur Springs during previous years, he stole the show in Steamboat, exhilarating approximately 2,000 onlookers with his winning jump of 119 feet. Howelsen first built a temporary ramp for the event on Woodchuck Hill, near the present site of Colorado Mountain College. The following winter he constructed a more permanent jumping platform across the river, on a hill above what was then a fenced-in elk refuge. He picked a north-facing slope that was steep and long enough for his jump and landing. The impact this display of initiative would have on the town is almost beyond description—affecting thousands of kids over the years, including over two dozen who would go on to become Olympic jumpers. Howelsen Hill, at a mere 440 vertical feet, remains the blue-collar little brother to the "Big Hill" of Mount Werner, but it has long attracted the same sort of love and admiration as the man who founded it. As Jean Wren so eloquently wrote in her book, *Steamboat Springs and the Treacherous and Speedy Skee*,

"The vital spark of enthusiasm that Carl

Howelsen brought with him into the isolated winter valley set fire to the energies of a whole community. He became the focus, the catalyst, that directed all the pent-up drive of a restless snowbound people out of doors. When he showed them skis and poles that would work better and set them free out on the tilted pastures that rimmed the town, he started a massive chain of events that would, in time, change the lives of their children, grandchildren and great-grandchildren."

"Everybody who came out of Steamboat Springs learned how to be a ski jumper first," said Jean's husband, Gordy Wren, in Smokey Vandergrift's video version of *The Treacherous and Speedy Skee*. Gordy was a fine jumper in his own right who was the area manager at Howelsen from 1949 to 1955. "Probably, being good ski jumpers is what made all of the Werners such good downhill skiers," Wren added, "Because they didn't worry too much about being in the air—they were used to it."

Opposite page: Captain Carl, showing proper form on landing, 1912.
Below: Howelsen, ready for a ski tour with Marjorie Perry (second from left) and other willing tourers.

Carl Howelsen

In late March 1909, Carl Howelsen stepped off a Denver train on the way to becoming one of the most influential outdoorsmen in the history of Colorado. He'd immigrated to Chicago from Norway in 1905 but had always dreamed of going even farther west, to the snow-covered slopes of the Rocky Mountains. When Howelsen finally moved west, he brought with him not only his bricklaying tools but also a passion for skiing that would lead him to introduce it to a state now almost synonymous with the sport.

Howelsen had a huge influence on skiing no matter where he went. While in Chicago, he helped fellow Norwegians form the famous Norge Ski Club, which promoted the sport extensively throughout the Midwest in the early 1900s. Howelsen also helped organize and promote many Chicago ski jumping exhibitions—a skill that would serve him well later in Colorado. But his most famous career move had nothing to do with being a bricklayer or a ski-club promoter. While making 60-foot exhibition jumps into a pool at Chicago's Riverview Amusement Park, Howelsen was approached by a representative of the Barnum & Bailey circus. A quick conversation led to a job offer, and in the summer of 1906, Carl Howelsen joined The Greatest Show on Earth, earning himself the title Captain Carl, the Flying Norseman.

Having quickly learned the value of capitalism in America, Howelsen asked for and received the then-unheard-of salary of $200 a week to become a "Ski Sailor." He signed a contract and set his premier performance for New York's Madison Square Garden at the opening show of Barnum & Bailey's 1907 season.

The 75-foot jump took place on March 21, in front of a sold-out Garden crowd of 20,000 awe-struck spectators.

Top: Carl Howelsen, father of Steamboat skiing.
Bottom: Carl with some of his early students.

Howelsen's performance drew rave reviews, and the Greatest Show on Earth then embarked on a grinding six-month tour, in which Howelsen performed twice a day in 146 cities in 16 states, often jumping over elephants. But eventually the odds caught up with him and, later that same year, Howelsen fell while climbing to the top of his jump. He hurt his back and was forced to quit the circus and return to Chicago and his masonry work.

But much like James Harvey Crawford more than a quarter of a century earlier, the mountainous West called to Howelsen, and two years later, he was getting off the train in Colorado. Also like Crawford, Howelsen wasn't satisfied with Denver. He was dying to see, and ski, the Front Range's western slope. So in December 1911, his back long healed, he joined fellow Norwegian Angell Schmidt on the train to Corona Pass—just east of present-day Winter Park—where they strapped on skis and toured 44 miles to Hot Sulphur Springs.

While there, the two met a Swiss man named John Peyer, who just happened to have organized a winter carnival that was taking place the next day. Though skiing wasn't originally planned to be part of the event, the two Norwegians built a jump, showed Peyer how far they could fly, and quickly convinced him that skiing should be included. The carnival was such a success that Hot Sulphur Springs held another later that same winter, and Howelsen and Schmidt made the trek again, only this time the Denver media heard about it. One headline read: "CARL HOWELSEN AND ANGELL SCHMIDT RETURN FROM TRIP IN MOUNTAINS AND WONDER WHY COLORADOANS ARE NOT SKI EXPERTS."

"Colorado ought to enjoy more exercise on skis," Howelsen said, as quoted in the article. "The snow here is light and dry and splendid for traveling. It doesn't ball up and pack, as the snow in Eastern states does. I've just come back from a trip over the range, and it is a splendid sport."

The winter ski carnival continued in Hot Sulphur Springs the following two years, and in February 1913, a Steamboat woman named Marjorie Perry was riding the train through town on her way back from Denver when some friends there told her she should stay the night because there was a ski jumping exhibition the following day. It was at this carnival that Miss Perry met Howelsen and suggested that he come to Steamboat and give one of his jumping exhibitions.

According to Leif Howelsen's book, *The Flying Norseman*, Carl found in Steamboat "what he was looking for in the United States." He soon bought a ranch in

Strawberry Park, and when winter came he naturally set about organizing a ski carnival for Steamboat. The Steamboat Springs Winter Carnival has taken place every February since and is the longest-running such event in the country.

In 1922, 13 years after arriving in Colorado and nine years after moving to Steamboat, Howelsen made a trip back to Oslo, Norway, for his parents' 50th wedding anniversary. He would never return. While there, he met and fell in love with a woman named Anna Skarstroen, who he eventually married. The couple had one son, Leif, who wrote a book about his father and who still makes occasional trips to Steamboat. Carl Howelsen continued to jump until the age of 71. He died in 1955, three years after his last leap on skis. ✑

An early promotional poster for the Barnum and Bailey Circus showing a somewhat exaggerated portrayal of Howelsen's jump.

Above: View of Howelsen Hill from downtown Steamboat, circa 1937.
Opposite page: The boat tow, an eight-passenger "lift" bounced over large piles of snow on the way up Howelsen Hill.

The Werner kids—Buddy, Loris and Skeeter—all learned to ski at Howelsen before going on to become Olympians. Their mother, Hazie Werner, ran the hot dog stand there with her sister for the Steamboat Springs Winter Sports Club (SSWSC). The SSWSC was founded in 1915, and though its main purpose was to train junior skiers and put on the winter carnival, the club also made sure that the record-breaking jumps at Howelsen were certified with the National Ski Association of America.

Longtime valley rancher and ski patrolman Vernon Summer remembers coming to watch the professional jumpers at Howelsen: "Every kid had skis here, and if there was a hill with a good slope on it, why, we'd build a ski jump. But when we went to town, to Howelsen, and saw those professionals soaring through the air like they did…boy, you just couldn't believe it."

By the 1920s, a set of bleachers had been built at Howelsen that would hold 150 spectators, and in 1931 a Denver ski instructor named Graeme McGowan was hired to teach downhill and slalom. But he wasn't hired by anyone in Steamboat. Rather, the Denver and Rio Grande Railroad footed the bill, figuring the investment would pay off in the form of more skiers taking the train into the mountains. The town of jumpers didn't think much at first of this new sport of slalom, with some spectators actually laughing at competitors during the first slalom race in 1933.

Despite this early opposition, by the mid '30s timber and brush had been cleared at Howelsen in order to add slalom and downhill runs on either side of the jumping area. In 1937, Howelsen became one of the first ski areas in the country to offer night skiing, though the source of light was mounted on the roof of a Lincoln Avenue building across the Yampa River. The following year, permanent electric lights were added just in time for the winter carnival, and people could ski Howelsen two nights a week. Also in 1938 came the boat tow—an eight-passenger lift that hauled skiers slowly up the hill at the rate of roughly 100 people an hour. As described by Jean Wren, the device was

"pulled by a cable on a pulley, looking more like an immense square rowboat, and rode most of the time with a vigorous bumping motion, as though it were being pulled up a staircase." Within five years, the original boat tow was replaced with a double boat that could haul twice as many skiers twice as far up the hill. This later model, which ran until 1970, consisted of two separate boats, each holding 10 people; when one was being pulled up the hill by the cable, the other would act as a counterweight on the way down.

"It'd knock your teeth out," says Paul Wegeman, who took many trips on the boat tow with his younger brother Keith, when both were training for future Olympic appearances. Adds Loris Werner: "The tram board now [the Colorado Passenger Tramway Safety Board] would have a fit if they ever saw what that thing was. If you were sitting in the back, you better stand up and hang on or it would launch you right out of there."

A rope tow was added in 1945, and by the following year, Howelsen Hill had a big log clubhouse and was hosting the

National Jumping Championships for the first time. The next four years saw the first of many massive fund-raising efforts at Howelsen, in part to rebuild the 90-meter jump but also to finance the purchase of what was to be the longest single-span ski lift in America. The lift, which featured 80 chairs and 20 T-bars, opened on January 31, 1948, and ran 1,440 feet from the base of Howelsen up to the top, down the other side and then up to the top of Emerald Mountain, the large, rolling peak located just behind Howelsen.

Loris Werner remembers some of the peculiarities of the old lift: "If you got on one of the chairs instead of one of the T-bars, you had to go all the way to the top of Emerald—you couldn't just get off at the top of Howelsen. But with the T-bar, you could get off at the top of Howelsen and ski down the back side. Then, if you were tall enough, you could reach one of the passing T-bars, pull it down, and ride up the rest of the way [to the top of Emerald]. But if you were a little short sucker like me, then you had to hook your poles together and time it just right so that you could jump up

Opposite page: Skiing on the east side of Howelsen Hill, mid 1950s.
Below: The ski sleigh, which brought skiers from the Harbor Hotel to Howelsen and also picked up train passengers at the train depot.

Howelsen Hill Records

Being the host site for dozens of various national championships over the years, Howelsen Hill has seen many bars set and records broken on its slopes. By 1972, the national distance-jumping record had been broken eight times on Howelsen's big hill. The first was in 1916, when Chicago's Ragnar Omtvedt (for whom the restaurant Ragnar's, at Steamboat ski area, is named) sailed 192 feet off the fledgling jump, which was still being rebuilt just about every year. The national record was broken on Howelsen again the next season, this time by a Steamboat local named Henry Hall. Hall's leap of 203 feet would be the last national distance record set at Howelsen for the next 33 years, until Gordy Wren's 297-foot leap during Steamboat's 1950 winter carnival. In fact, the national distance record was shattered four times on that one February day—twice by Wren himself, who not only broke his own record but became the first American to surpass the 300-foot barrier, with a leap of 301.

Wren's performances, which took place on the new Graham jump—named for local utilities magnate Douglas Graham, who

contributed thousands of dollars to its construction—were followed by a 305-foot jump by Merrill Barber. Barber's distance was then promptly bested by Art Devlin, who was the last to break the national record that day, with a distance of 307. Art Tokle actually jumped 311, but was disqualified when he, as Jean Wren writes, "fell in a smashing, clattering, tumble of skis, arms and legs." Devlin's record didn't stand long either. The flurry of record breaking on Howelsen ended the following year, in 1951, when Ansten Samuelstuen launched 316 feet, becoming the last to set a national distance record at Howelsen until Gene Kotlarek recorded a 318-footer there 12 years later.

Since 1963, the national record has been broken only once on Howelsen—in 1978 by Steamboat resident Jim Denney, with a leap of 354 feet. That record was made considerably more memorable, however, considering that it took place at the new $1 million jumping complex. ⚘

Above: Ragnar Omtvedt, 1916 World Champion.
Below: Steamboat's Henry Hall, 1917.

Art Devlin, with his national record-setting 307-foot leap, Winter Carnival, 1950.

Above: Gordy Wren, teaching at Howelsen Hill, 1951. Future Olympians Moose Barrows and Jere Elliott are fifth and sixth from right, respectively. Right: The first chairlift at Howelsen, which included 80 chairs and 20 T-bars, was briefly the longest single-span chairlift in North America.

and grab the bar with the poles when it came by. Sometimes it'd jerk you off the ground and spin you around. Then it took so long to get to the top that sometimes you'd have to take a whiz in the track on the way up."

At that time, there was only a small crew of employees who worked at Howelsen, so everybody chipped in with all the jobs that needed to be done. "There was no defined, 'this person did this and this person did that,'" says Werner. "I remember one guy named Marvin Rice. He checked tickets, ran the boat tow, ran the T-bar, worked with Gordy on various projects. He kicked me off the mountain about once a week for going too fast or screwing around or whatever, telling me, 'You get to hike for a few days, son.'"

Werner also remembers the joint effort it took to keep Howelsen in skiable shape before they had snowmaking and grooming machines. "The only way we maintained it was by hand, so it was a community effort," he says. "We had to get this big hill in shape, so the Lion's Club and the Kiwanis and everybody else, they'd show up at night and

we'd do what we called 'snow the hill.' You'd shovel snow out into the troughs and boot pack it in. Hell, it might take us a week to get to where we could ski it. Now they just turn on a hose and a gun and run their little machine up there."

While many people have played a role in the colorful history of Howelsen Hill, nobody—with the possible exception of Al Wegeman, who was the first Howelsen Hill Manager, from 1944 to 1949—has impacted the mountain and the kids who skied there like Gordy Wren. After serving seven years as a climbing and ski mountaineering instructor for the 10th Mountain Division, partly at Camp Hale in Colorado and partly in Italy, Wren returned to Steamboat in 1949 and became mountain manager at Howelsen. He wasted no time before becoming involved in various projects, including joining Ed "Pop" Werner and others in building a downhill run that ran from the top of Emerald Mountain to the river.

"It was a little dangerous," says Moose Barrows, who raced there on several occasions before going on to compete in the Olympic downhill in 1968. "You went *right* past the

Above: The smoldering 90-meter jump at Howelsen, May 1972.
Opposite page: Future Olympians Keith (left) and Paul Wegeman, 1951.

rock quarry—I mean within 10 feet of it—and the Steilhang was right above it. If you made the wrong turn up there, you'd go right off into space."

The downhill run, originally proposed by the local American Legion as a memorial for Steamboat residents killed in the war, was only one of many ideas the team of Pop Werner and Gordy Wren guided to fruition on Howelsen. In 1950, the pair helped found two popular and promising events: the Howelsen Hill Invitational Training Camp—an intense two-week instructional clinic that ran for 11 years and helped prepare many young jumpers for international competition—and the Fourth of July summer ski jumping exhibitions, where up to 1,000 spectators would watch a couple dozen jumpers ski down 40 tons of ice shavings and land in a huge pile of straw.

Olympian Marvin Crawford was also heavily involved with various activities on Howelsen. "I worked on and off with the kids jumping program, and I was always involved with the meets," he says. "I did the P.A. announcing for years and, like everybody else, I'd work all night, sometimes trying to get the hills in shape for the competitions. Howelsen Hill, when we were juniors, is where we did all of our skiing. And we competed against Aspen, who had the big mountain, but we usually didn't have any trouble beating them even though all we had was 400 feet of Howelsen."

In 1959, Howelsen Hill went through one of its dozens of remodelings: Under the supervision of local rancher

John Fetcher, a new jumping platform was built to FIS specifications, making Howelsen one of only four complexes in North America to offer an official 90-meter jump. Sadly, this jump burned to the ground on May 19, 1972. Several theories exist as to what caused the fire—everything from carelessness by employees to negligence by people camping under the ramp to arson by anti-Olympic protestors (Howelsen Hill was the designated site for all Nordic events in a failed bid by the Denver Olympic Committee to bring the 1976 Olympics to Colorado). But whatever caused the jump to burn down, Fetcher, who by this time had played a significant role in the development of Steamboat ski area, was determined to rebuild it.

Fetcher spent the next four years working with volunteers like Wren, Crawford, Marvin Elkins and Billy Kidd, raising money to rebuild the complex, only to have a mudslide in 1976 come down Howelsen and demolish the area where the new ramp was being built. Nevertheless, by January 1978, the North American Ski Jumping Championships were held at the new Howelsen Hill complex, and the judges' tower was named Fetcher Tower. By

Marvin Crawford at the microphone with local investor Marcellus Merrill, February 1968.

Though he was never a coach or a serious competitor, few individuals have influenced skiing in Steamboat like John Fetcher. He moved to the Yampa Valley from Philadelphia in the fall of 1949, 14 years after graduating from Harvard Business and Engineering Schools. An Illinois native, Fetcher left his job as Chief Plant Engineer for the Budd Company in Philly, and arrived in Steamboat with his wife, Criss, their family, and his brother Stan's family. Together they bought the 2,600-acre Angostura Ranch in the Elk River Valley, just south of Clark.

"It was pretty tough for us up there the first few years," Fetcher says. "Harvard never taught me how to shoe a horse, and I wasn't even sure which end of the cow to feed."

Fetcher had grown up skiing and even invented what was likely one of the first sets of metal skis. They were

Top: John Fetcher: rancher, entrepreneur, businessman.
Bottom: A common winter sight: Fetcher getting off the chairlift. Even at 90 years old, Fetcher retains his membership in the National Ski Patrol.

only used once, in the spring of 1938 at Tuckerman Ravine in New Hampshire. (After bending one ski, he gave the other one to the Dartmouth Ski Museum.) His interest in skiing was one of the main reasons Fetcher settled in the Yampa Valley, and he quickly became immersed in Steamboat's love of the sport, especially after meeting coach and competitor Gordy Wren.

"Gordy got me involved with the Winter Sports Club, particularly the jumping hill," Fetcher says. He went on to use his considerable engineering skills to design ski jumps at a variety of resorts including Park City, Crested Butte, Winter Park and Aspen.

Though Fetcher played a major role in the creation of Storm Mountain Ski Area, Steamboat Ski Resort's original name, even then he always had more than one project going. "That man has had his fingers in a little bit of everything," says Merle Nash, who worked with Fetcher during the early years at the ski area. "After a while the rest of us would get kind of burnt out on doing all this stuff. But John never did. Whether it was with water, Mount Werner or Howelsen—he's been a pusher every inch of the way."

Steve Elkins, a man who worked for Fetcher during the early days of the Steamboat Ski Resort, agrees. "If it weren't for John, we wouldn't have the facility we have at Howelsen today, that's for sure," Elkins says. "He would just keep working on projects long after everybody else would have quit. And he always had a way of squeezing a little more money or work out of you. I remember how he always used to talk us into working on a Saturday and just donating the time. He'd look at you after you worked all week and say something like, 'Well, we really need to get this done and we really can't afford to pay you, but, you know, if you guys wanted to you could come help out.' And we'd all be back up there on Saturday, looking at each other wondering how he talked us into it."

Fetcher's work for the Storm Mountain Ski Area is legendary, particularly his 1962 run out to California with his farm truck to pick up a couple of bullwheels for the first chairlift. Nevertheless, it was his tireless efforts toward Howelsen Hill and local water projects that gained him much admiration and respect. In the mid '60s, Fetcher sold 600 acres of his ranch to the Colorado Game and Fish Department, a move that led to the creation of Steamboat Lake. He was also the man behind the building of the Yamcolo Reservoir southwest of Yampa, and the Stagecoach

Reservoir 16 miles southeast of Steamboat.

"I am particularly proud of those water storage projects," Fetcher says.

The Fetcher Tower at Howelsen bears his name because of the tremendous fundraising effort he led to get the complex built in the mid '70s. He was also an Olympic jumping referee at the 1972 Games in Sapporo, Japan, and the 1980 Games in Lake Placid, New York.

At 91 years of age, Fetcher remains a member of the National Ski Patrol and can be found today continuing his work as the secretary and manager for the Upper Yampa Water Conservancy and as manager of the Mount Werner Water and Sanitation District, which he helped create in 1966. If you swing by his office and he's not there, you might want to check the slopes or the tennis courts. ♪

John Fetcher skis through the ribbon at Howelsen Hill during the North American Ski Jumping Championships dedication ceremonies, January 1978.

Howelsen remains the oldest ski area in continuous operation in the state of Colorado.

then, the city had taken over ownership and operation of Howelsen, and it remains the oldest ski area in continuous operation in the state of Colorado.

"Howelsen Hill contributes in large part to the unique nature of this community," says local historian Jayne Hill. "You have kids who aren't just out there having fun for a day but are really training to be world-class athletes. It's a big part of what makes this a serious skiing community."

During a warm spring day in 1993, the Howelsen Hill lodge collapsed onto itself, leaving nothing but a huge pile of wood where the building was standing only minutes before. Since the lodge served as the headquarters of the Winter Sports Club, and since the accident occurred during the middle of the day, the whole town felt lucky that nobody was inside the building when it tumbled to the ground. The lodge was rebuilt later that summer, and today Howelsen Hill and the Winter Sports Club continue to produce athletes at the highest ranks of the sport: Tim Tetreault, three-time Olympian and three-time U.S. Nordic combined champion; Todd Lodwick, three-time Olympian with a dozen Nordic Combined World Cup podiums; Shannon Dunn, Olympic gold medalist in snowboarding; Travis Mayer, Olympic silver medalist in moguls; alpine racers Caroline LaLive and Matt Grosjean; freestyler Ann Battelle—the list goes on and on. In 1995, Lodwick, a Steamboat native, did something no American had done in 11 years—he won a Nordic Combined World Cup event. He went on to win three more, and along with fellow Nordic Combined team members Carl Van Loan, Bill Demong, Johnny Spillane and Nathan Gearhart, narrowly missed the podium at the 2002 Olympics, finishing fourth.

The jumping team is also strong, anchored by veteran Alan Alborn, who finished 11th in Salt Lake, and Clint Jones, who became the youngest U.S. ski champion in history when he came in first on the K-120 jump in March 2000, at the age of 15. Other jumping-team members include Tommy Schwall and Brendan Doran, the U.S. 90-meter champion in 2000.

The Howelsen Hill complex now consists of a sprawling, 150-acre playground that includes 20-, 30-, 50-, 70-, 90- and 120-meter jumps, as well as a covered ice rink, halfpipe, Nordic trails, rodeo grounds, four lighted softball fields (host to the annual Triple Crown National Softball Championships), horse stables, soccer and rugby fields, tennis, basketball and volleyball courts, an alpine slide and a skateboard park. Carl Howelsen would be honored. ✳

Opposite page: Winter Carnival celebration, February 2002.
Below: Catching some air at the Howelsen halfpipe.

Chapter 3

Storm Mountain

Storm Mountain in 1959, showing the two trails—eventually called
Voo Doo and See Me—that were cut before the first lift was built.

James Temple was a multifaceted man in the mid 1950s. He was a third-generation Colorado rancher who had grown up making hay and feeding cows on his family's Focus Ranch along the Wyoming-Colorado border. He was a World War II veteran who had served in intelligence operations aboard the U.S.S. Higby. After the war he had been a ski instructor at the Jack Reddish Ski School in Brighton, Utah. Then he'd been a patroller for seven years at Sun Valley, Idaho, where he rose to assistant head of ski patrol and lead avalanche forecaster. And he was a husband and father of four, having married Audrey Light in 1951, granddaughter of Steamboat's most famous merchant, F.M. Light.

But most of all, Jim Temple was a believer. And by 1955, after years of dreaming about it, there was nothing he believed in more than the idea of building a ski resort on Storm Mountain, now called Mount Werner. "I knew I wanted to build a resort, so I started studying mountains all the way from Montana to New Mexico," Temple says. "But in

Jim Temple on one of his many horseback trips up Storm Mountain, in the late 1950s. He also led snowcat trips on the mountain.

Olympian Buddy Werner (left) and Jim Temple, spring 1956.

the end, I narrowed it down to Peak One, over by Frisco [Colorado], and Storm Mountain. Ultimately, I decided on Storm in my home county, because it had all the ingredients to at least match Sun Valley, if not be better."

At the end of the 1955–56 season, Temple left Sun Valley for good and returned to his native Steamboat, where he began taking horseback reconnaissance trips to the top of Storm Mountain with a Forest Service supervisor and various friends, conducting his own feasibility study for building a resort.

"Nobody really thought Storm could be a viable ski mountain," says John Fetcher, one of Temple's original partners in the Storm Mountain Ski Area. "Everybody thought it was too far from Denver."

But Temple wasn't deterred. He led a group of skiers

The original Storm Mountain brochure, 1959.

Above: Smith Ranch and the base of Storm Mountain, winter, 1958. Opposite page: The original visionaries, groundbreaking, July 4, 1958: Front row (left to right): Jim Temple, Buddy Werner, Marvin Crawford, Bill Sayre, John Fetcher. Standing: Willis Nash and Glen Stukey.

from the Winter Sports Club up Storm Mountain on snowcats in April 1956, and he made a surveying trip to the top later that spring with Buddy and Loris Werner. Temple also started using the now-famous term "champagne powder" to promote Steamboat's light, dry snow. (He credits Kremmling, Colorado, rancher Joe McElroy for the phrase.) By the fall of '57, Temple was taking jeep trips to the top of Buffalo Pass and across to Storm, sharing his ideas and visualizing how his mountain would take shape.

"I guess I considered just about anybody I skied the mountain with at that time to be a potential business partner," he says. "But I was mostly looking for people who wanted to ski and wanted to be involved on the mountain."

By January 1958, he'd found enough fellow believers to form Storm Mountain Corp., with the goal of building a ski area. Temple, 32, was president. John Fetcher, 47, was first vice president and chief engineer. Marvin Crawford, 28, who had competed in the Olympic jumping and Nordic Combined events two years earlier in Cortina, Italy, was second vice president. Gerald Groswold, 28, whose family manufactured Groswold skis in Denver (and who later became president of Winter Park) was secretary and legal counsel. William Sayre, 38, from Denver, was company architect.

Less than a month later, Temple started selling off portions of his stake in his family's Focus Ranch, using the money to purchase land at the base of Storm Mountain.

After he bought 200 acres from C.C. and Stella Craig in an area known as Bear Claw just east of modern-day Ski Time Square, he made an offer on a 100-acre parcel directly beneath where the gondola now runs. But the owner, Ernest Arnold, wasn't interested—not for cash, anyway.

"I kept talking to him, every month, and he kept putting me off," Temple says. "So finally I said, 'Well, you need a tractor, don't you?' So old Ernie ended up with my tractor."

The official groundbreaking ceremony for Storm Mountain Ski Area occurred on July 6, 1958, and trail clearing continued throughout the summer, with most of the work being done by Temple himself and two men he'd hired, chainsaw operator Norm Sandelin and cat driver Jess Brenton. "Willis Nash owned a [Caterpillar] D-7, and I made a deal with him to use that cat for two or three summers, in exchange for stock in the company," Temple says. "Then I hired Jess Brenton—who was 75 at the time—to do most of the clearing. He was the oldest cat operator in the world, I think."

It would be three years before the first lift went up, but that didn't keep Steamboat's ski-hungry residents from testing out the new runs. Both Steamboat High School and the University of Wyoming hosted races on what are now the See Me and Voo Doo trails during the winters of '58, '59 and '60, after Brenton bulldozed a road to the top so jeeps could bring racers back up.

Temple eventually secured options on 827 acres at the base of the fledgling resort, including one parcel (the Smith

Brush burning on Storm Mountain, 1958, on what would eventually become Voo Doo, one of the first of two trails on the mountain.

Ranch) that he bought only after the owner saw the bulldozers moving in. "She saw the cats and decided she didn't want to stay," Temple says. "That's how close we were cutting it—we didn't have that ranch yet, but we were starting to build the resort. We'd have been skiing down to her fence line if she wouldn't have sold."

Like most ski area developments at the time—or since—shortage of money was a constant problem. Crawford and Fetcher had each made small loans to the company, but nobody big had come forward. Consequently, Temple made dozens of trips to Denver looking for backing, and it was on one of these trips that he met a 33-year-old investment broker named Henry "Hank" Perry with Bosworth, Sullivan and Co.

"He just walked into my office one morning," Perry says. "And told me he wanted to build a ski resort."

Perry and Groswold helped Temple create a second corporate entity in April 1959 called Storm Mountain Ski Corp.

Opposite page: University of Wyoming racers on Storm Mountain, 1959. Below: Jess Brenton, the oldest cat operator in the world, on the Caterpillar D-7.

Naturally, competing with Aspen and Vail was a major theme of Steamboat's early promotional efforts. As early as 1965, the company was buying billboard space in Denver and putting up ads that read, "THERE IS NO ASPEN. SKI STEAMBOAT." In 1982, the marketing department came up with a slogan that said, "Steamboat: more mountain than Aspen, more powder than Vail, more lifts than Snowmass, more Sun than Sun Valley, more bars than Utah."

Rod Hanna was the public relations director at the time, and he remembers the idea behind the campaign. "Whenever I'd get a journalist up here, we'd be on the chairlift and come up over yet another big area of the mountain and inevitably the comment was, 'My God, I had no idea this place was so big.' Because you couldn't see it from the road, everybody thought we were just this little old ski resort in northwest Colorado. We had to get the message out that we were a major resort. And I think that campaign did it."

The idea was taken even further a couple years later, after Hanna and then–marketing director Kent Myers found themselves with a camera during a particularly crowded day at Vail. "We took a picture of their lift line," Hanna says. "Which of course was out the maze and

A T-shirt proudly displaying one of Steamboat's early marketing campaigns.

magazine ads with the headline, 'WE WON'T GIVE YOU THE SAME OLD LINE.' It only ran for a few months before [Vail executive] Andy Daly blew his top and asked us to pull it. We were pretty aggressive in those years."

But the first aggressive ad campaign may have been the billboards from 1965. Marvin Crawford fondly remembers that first attempt to lure Denver skiers away from Aspen and toward Steamboat: "We were trying to get business from the Front Range, so we had those billboards all over Denver. It was a great campaign, and even Aspen got on the bandwagon because, of course, it benefited them as well."

But in 1966, the winter after the signs started appearing, Aspen figured out a way to get even. "The Aspen Ski Club invited Skeeter Werner and me over to be king and queen of the Aspen Winterskol, a celebration they had every winter," Crawford says. "[Actor] Kirk Douglas was supposed to have been the king, and he couldn't make it. So, because of this advertising campaign and the fact that I was manager of the area, they asked me to substitute. So Skeeter and I rode down the main street of Aspen in a horse-drawn sled, and they hung a sign on the back of the sleigh that said, 'THERE

King and queen of Aspen's Winterskol: Marv Crawford and Skeeter Werner.

Together they wrote a prospectus for selling stock in the company. Their goal was to raise enough money to operate existing facilities, build a poma lift and double chairlift and pay back company officials like Temple, Fetcher and Crawford. Unfortunately, the stock sale raised less than $100,000—not nearly enough.

"We were trying to find an underwriter on 17th Street [the financial district in Denver], but they wanted us to wait a few months and we needed capital right away," Temple says. "I must've gone to Denver several times a week for two years, working with Groswold and Perry. I'd drive down there and work until two in the morning and then drive home. Sometimes it'd be daylight when I'd get back to Steamboat."

Despite the money shortage, Storm Mountain opened on December 22, 1961, with a poma lift on Cub Claw (roughly where the Southface lift is today) that carried skiers 272 vertical feet up to the top of the Headwall. Profit for the season was $265. Temple was pleased to see his dream

materialize, but he knew he was going to need a lot more money to keep it going, so again he turned to Perry.

"He told me he could find private investors," Temple says. "All he needed was a percentage of the company. So we made a deal."

On July 20, 1962, Temple and Perry entered into a trust agreement that gave Perry 50,000 shares and voting control of more than 50 percent of the stock in Storm Mountain Ski Corp. for a period of eight years. In exchange, Temple agreed to resign his position as president and Perry agreed to "secure for Storm Mountain, sufficient funds for operation of the ski area, at least for the ski season of 1962–63" and, additionally, "cause completion of the acquisition and installation of the now partially completed chairlift at said ski area." The relationship would prove disastrous, leading to almost two years of legal battling over Storm Mountain.

The seeds for the court fight had been planted the previous year, eight months before the trust agreement had even

Opposite page: Skiers riding to the top of the Headwall via the area's first lift, the Cub Claw poma.
Below: The poster promoting Storm Mountain's opening day.

Below, top: Pointing the way to Storm Mountain, 1961.
Below, bottom: Hank Perry, the partner with the fundraising talent.

been signed. Perry had already gone looking for money and had found it in the form of three major investors: Denver physician Mack Clayton, Denver banker John McCready and Mary Helen Stewart, a member of the Shamrock, Texas, oil family that founded the Diamond Shamrock gas stations and convenience stores now scattered throughout the West.

Perry and his three investors, along with Fetcher, Crawford and Merle Nash (Willis Nash's son) had formed a company in November 1961 called the Steamboat Partnership, with the idea of reorganizing and refinancing Storm Mountain Ski Corp. Temple, who had moved to Boulder with his family to find work, was not only left out of the partnership but was kept in the dark about it for almost two years. "The people providing the money didn't want Temple involved," Perry says.

Meanwhile, work had started on the Bear Claw double chairlift. The problem was that not all the parts were in Steamboat. Temple had ordered it from California businessman Paul Hunsiker, but part of the lift was at Big Bear Ski Resort and part of it was at Hunsiker's shop—Cowelco

Inc.—in Long Beach. Cowelco was facing financial difficulties itself and couldn't deliver, so—as would become a common theme in Steamboat throughout the years—it was John Fetcher to the rescue. Fetcher drove out to California in his flatbed farm truck with his neighbor Chuck Uhlein, and they loaded the two 12-foot bullwheels, and as much of the lift as they could fit, onto his truck for the trip back to Steamboat. "The bullwheels were originally intended for a gondola," Fetcher explains, "which is why they were much larger in diameter than necessary for a double chairlift."

Fetcher was forced to angle the bullwheels at 30 degrees on his truck's bed because they were too tall to pass through highway underpasses on the trip home and too wide to sit flat. When they got the bullwheels back to Steamboat, they had to rush to get the cable ready for the imminent opening. Despite the setbacks, Storm Mountain Ski Area officially opened (again) on January 12, 1963, with its new double chairlift up and running. Hank Perry says that one of the few arguments he and John Fetcher ever had took place

Opposite page: Putting up towers for the ski area's first lifts was always a team effort.
Below: To get the giant bullwheels onto his farm truck, John Fetcher had to angle them at 30 degrees.

Above: Ralph Selch's snack bar occupied the top floor of the A-frame. Opposite page: The Storm Hut A-frame opened in December 1962.

over the price of an opening-day lift ticket. "I wanted to charge $3.75, and John insisted that it be $3.25," Perry says. "He won that argument so that's what we charged." There was only one problem: Nobody showed up to pay it.

The temperature had dipped to 30 below zero and people stayed hunkered down in their Steamboat homes. "We only had one customer that first day," Fetcher says. "And Hank Perry backed into him in the parking lot. There was one single car in the whole lot, and Hank managed to hit it."

Even with the anemic skier numbers, commercial enterprises began to sprout at the base of the mountain. By Christmas 1962, an A-frame known as Storm Hut had been erected. Ralph Selch ran a snack bar upstairs, and siblings Buddy and Skeeter Werner turned the downstairs into the area's first ski shop, offering both retail and rental equipment. (Werner's Storm Hut later moved downtown, where it operated for over 20 years.) The hut also served as a warming shelter for up to 250 skiers.

Gradually, people did come out to see and ski the new area, with almost 3,000 skier visits recorded by the end of the season. Not that there weren't challenges. "Five of us traded off running that first lift," Fetcher says. "We didn't even bother with a top attendant. We just told people, 'Well, if you don't get off, you'll come back down again.' And some did."

But there was already bigger trouble brewing. Because of the shortage of funds, the Steamboat Partnership had borrowed $70,000 from the Routt County National Bank to keep the resort running, and the group had placed chattel mortgages on both lifts in order to pay a mechanic's lien—both actions in violation of the trust agreement between Perry and Temple. On November 9, 1963, Fetcher sent a letter to shareholders of the Storm Mountain Ski Corp. (which Temple says he never received, despite owning almost 65,000 shares), explaining that "a group known as the Steamboat Partnership, headed by Henry Perry, has loaned the company funds and has asked to be reimbursed for the monies previously advanced. The reimbursement amounts to $122,000. The monies advanced are secured by a chattel mortgage on the poma lift and the chairlift. If Storm Mountain Ski Corporation cannot meet this payment, it will not be able to hold title to the lifts or continue in business as the operator of the ski area." Later that month, the Steamboat Partnership foreclosed on Storm Mountain Ski Corp.

Then on November 21, 1963, Jim Temple sued Perry, Fetcher and the Steamboat Partnership, on behalf of himself

The first chairlift, Bear Claw, in 1963. Later, it was painted blue and yellow and renamed Christie. It was replaced entirely by the Christie III in 1979.

and the stockholders of Storm Mountain Ski Corp., causing the Boulder District Court to place a temporary restraining order on all activity related to the company. The court stated that "the defendant, Henry Perry, has a direct financial interest in the Steamboat Partnership and is the trustee in the Storm Mountain Corp., wherein he agreed not to transfer assets out of the corporation without consent of the plaintiff [Temple]."

His involvement in the case caused Perry to lose his seat on the New York Stock Exchange and his job at Bosworth, Sullivan. "The New York Stock Exchange has a law that says you cannot be part of another company without them being fully advised as to your involvement," Perry says. "I didn't feel like this was a big deal, so I didn't tell the New York Stock Exchange that I was trying to raise money for a ski area in Steamboat. But when it hit the front page of *The Denver Post*, my boss saw it."

The case dragged on for months, in part because of several motions to dismiss by Perry's attorneys. On July 28, Judge Marvin Foote ruled that Perry's motion to dismiss was

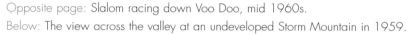

Opposite page: Slalom racing down Voo Doo, mid 1960s.
Below: The view across the valley at an undeveloped Storm Mountain in 1959.

Colorado Mountain College has one of the best backyards any student could ask for.

Higher Education

One of the often forgotten strengths of Steamboat Springs is the opportunities it affords in the classroom—rare for a small mountain town. Colorado Mountain College offers a two-year Associate of Arts or Associate of Science degree, as well as a variety of other programs, including business, environmental education and ski resort management. Lowell Whiteman prep school, on the other hand, offers both boarding and day classes for grades 9–12 and pioneered what is now known as "experiential education"—the idea of mixing academics with a wide variety of experiences, especially travel, that the students wouldn't otherwise experience in their home environments.

Both schools got their start about the same time that Storm Mountain Ski Area was being created. In 1962, a woman named Lucille Bogue—who had long dreamed of bringing higher education to Steamboat—persevered to create what was then a private liberal arts school called Yampa Valley College.

"What pleases me as much as anything is the fact that, despite its growth and modernization, [the school] still retains the concern and attention to the individual needs of each student, truly the hallmark of a small college," wrote Bogue in her book, *Miracle on a Mountain, The Story of a College*.

Yampa Valley College changed its name to Colorado Alpine College in 1966 and was purchased three years later by the United States International University, based in California. Yet the college continued to struggle for accreditation and enrollment, and by the late '70s the campus was in jeopardy of being leveled for condos. But an election in May 1981 brought the college under the publicly funded

The Lowell Whiteman School has helped produce many of the town's Olympians.

umbrella of the Colorado Mountain College (CMC) system that already had campuses in Leadville and Glenwood Springs, leading to a successful arrangement that has kept the college strong for the past 20 years.

Students at CMC (often jokingly referred to as "See Me Ski" by people other than tuition-paying parents), can choose from such programs as resort management or health/fitness technology, and they often find part-time work or internships on the mountain or in town that help them combine real-world experience with classroom studies. Currently, some 1,500 students attend Colorado Mountain College's Alpine Campus each year.

The Lowell Whiteman School was founded in 1957 as a small college prep school. It is named after Routt County native Lowell Whiteman, who started a summer camp in 1946 in Strawberry Park—sort of a boys' version of Perry-Mansfield.

The coed population at Lowell-Whiteman remains at about 50 each year, just like it was in the '60s. Some of the students train with the Steamboat Springs Winter Sports Club and Lowell Whiteman has helped produce 14 Olympic athletes, including Ryan Heckman, Dave Jarret, Maria Quintana, Tommy Schwall, Clint Jones, Caroline Lalive and 2002 silver-medal-winner Travis Mayer. When mud season comes to town, Lowell Whiteman students leave Steamboat for the school's notorious Foreign Trip—a tradition dating back to the school's founding—which in 2002 took them to places like Mexico, Greenland, Viet Nam.

Sadly, Lowell Whiteman passed away in May of 2002, at the age of 83. But his school and his lifelong dream of education in the outdoors lives on. ✒

Buddy Werner's death in an avalanche in Switzerland in the spring of 1964 devastated the entire town. The following year the resort changed its name to Mt. Werner Ski Area.

"granted in part and denied in part." The judge ruled that "while [Temple's] claim appears sound in fraud, it contains no allegations that the corporation [Storm Mountain] had funds with which to pay its debts."

The court granted Temple 60 days to file an amended complaint, essentially agreeing to transfer the assets back into Storm Mountain Ski Corp. and reinstate him as president if he could come up with the money to pay off the $122,000 demand note to the Steamboat Partnership. But Temple couldn't pay it. "I was mostly broke by that time," he says. "I still owned some land, but I'd sold most of that, too, to fight the case." Nevertheless, Temple says he met with Joe Coors, Jr., of the Coors Brewing family, who had agreed to put up the money until Coors' father talked him out of it. This was the last roll of the dice for Temple, who was forced to walk away from the resort he'd founded.

"I ran a ski area for five years, and I signed a trust agreement and lost it all," Temple says. "I trusted people, and that was dumb."

Local historian Jean Wren said she felt that Temple never received enough credit for founding the ski area. "I don't think there would be a resort out there today if it weren't for Jim Temple," she said. "But as so often happens, the person who gets something going gets plowed under in the process. Jim didn't know how to play with the big boys. And John Fetcher did."

"I know there were some hard feelings about what happened," says Crawford, himself an officer of both Storm Mountain Ski Corp. and the Steamboat Partnership, "but Temple just wanted too big a piece of the pie. He did a lot of work putting that thing together initially, but when it became necessary to raise capital to keep the company going, he wanted to take controlling interest. And there was just no way that was going to happen."

As a testament to his drive and determination—and despite all the battles that took place over Storm Mountain—by the time Temple moved his family down to Boulder, he was already looking at trying to develop another ski area, at Peak One near Frisco. "And I almost died!" says his wife, Audrey. "I said, 'Oh, no, not another one.'" (Temple eventually dropped the Peak One project.)

That year, 1964, turned out to be tough for the entire community of Steamboat Springs. On April 12, hometown hero and Olympic star Buddy Werner, 28, was killed in an avalanche while filming a ski movie near St. Moritz, Switzerland. The small town was devastated. "I don't think there was a person in Steamboat who wasn't deeply affected by his death," says Crawford, an Olympic teammate of Buddy's earlier that same year. "It was a very difficult time." Storm Mountain was renamed Mount Werner, and the following year the resort changed its name to Mt. Werner Ski Area.

Fetcher asked Crawford, who was then living in Denver, if he'd be interested in returning to Steamboat to take over as mountain manager. "I remember when my wife and I first talked about moving back to Steamboat," Crawford says. "It was on the way home from Buddy's funeral, and it was a big decision for me because I had a good job with IBM in Denver and I had three kids. As it turned out, it was the right decision, because Steamboat is such a great place to raise a family. We had one chairlift my first year [the Bear Claw double, later named Christie], and one poma—and if we had 200 skiers on a weekend, then we were doing pretty good."

Despite skier visits climbing to nearly 12,000 by the end of the season, financial difficulties still overwhelmed the young company. "I remember driving up to John Fetcher's ranch to brainstorm about problems," Crawford says. "I'd go up there a couple times a week just so we could go over everything. Hank Perry was in Denver trying to raise more money and get people interested, and John was up here hawking his cattle just to make payroll—it got to that point."

Another reorganization led to the formation of two separate companies in November 1963—Winterland Engineering and the Steamboat Land Co. Winterland Engineering, under the leadership of Fetcher, ran the ski hill, while Steamboat Land Co., under the direction of Perry and Indianapolis coal magnate Harrison Eiteljorg, developed the real estate. It was

Eiteljorg who had the Mt. Werner Lodge built in 1967.

An octagon building that housed the ski patrol and maintenance shop went up in 1965, but both it and the A-frame were torn down nine years later. Also in 1965, the Forest Service gave approval for the Thunderhead lift, the first lift onto public land. "I had no problem dealing with the Forest Service," Fetcher says. "I just went in and asked for the permit, and a few weeks later we had it." Thunderhead was built later that year, with a Small Business Administration (SBA) loan. Many of the trails serviced by the Thunderhead lift were cut by local kids. Olympian Jim "Moose" Barrows, who was in college at the time, remembers the work well. "I'm not even talking chainsaws—I mean by hand, with axes and saws."

In 1967, the company secured another SBA loan with the help of Mix Beauvais, who joined the company from Jackson Hole Ski Resort at the urging of Hank Perry and John Fetcher. Says Beauvais: "There were four lifts when I arrived, and you could see all the skiing from the bottom." Beauvais

The Octagon building housed the ski patrol and a maintenance shop until 1970. For a time it was a restaurant called The Point. It was torn down in 1974.

and Fetcher took several trips to Denver's Central Bank to ask for money. "We had to get special permission to park because we had John's rickety old farm truck that wouldn't fit through the bank gate. We wore overalls and looked like a couple of sheepherders coming to borrow money."

Crawford resigned as mountain manager in 1967 in order to pursue other business interests, but not before first filling his own shoes by making a trip to Jackson Hole and convincing Gordy Wren to come down and fill the position. "Gordy was a little hesitant at first because they were already pretty well established up there," Crawford says about the Wyoming recruiting visit. "But he finally decided that this is what he wanted to do—move back to Steamboat, where he grew up."

Wren was already a Steamboat legend, both as a skier and a coach, the only American ever to qualify for all four ski disciplines in the same Olympics—alpine, jumping, cross-country and Nordic combined. As mountain manager, Wren oversaw the construction of both the Four Points and

Below: Gordy Wren, home again in 1967.
Opposite page: Hurricane, cut in the late '60s, bumped up and ready to go.

"We wore overalls and looked like a couple of sheepherders coming to borrow money."

Burgess Creek lifts in 1968–69, as well as all the weather-themed trails like White Out, Twister, Hurricane and Blizzard that descend from the two lifts.

By 1969, skiing had become a billion-dollar industry, but Fetcher and company were ready to move on. "Hank [Perry] and I just didn't have the wherewithal financially. We knew we needed to put in a gondola. And to finance it, we knew we needed some big money." Several parties had shown interest in buying the ski area. But the group that showed the most promise was LTV Aerospace, a subsidiary of Ling-Temco-Vought Corp., out of Dallas.

In November 1969, the Storm Mountain Ski Corp. was sold to LTV Aerospace for a reported $4 million. By then, because of all the transactions that had taken place over the previous dozen years, lots of people were shareholders. "There were probably 30 to 50 shareholders, because every time we sold a lot, the buyer would get a share in the company and a lifetime pass or something," says Beauvais. "The people who held onto their LTV stock did very well because it was a big company going through a growth pattern, just like a lot of companies were in those days."

Some of the people who hung onto their lifetime passes also did well. In the early '90s, after Merle Nash's father passed away, Merle and other family members were gathered around a big table going over the contents of an old safety deposit box that had been left at the bank. And there, inside a manila envelope, under a bunch of old stock certificates, they found 16 lifetime ski passes. "I brought them over to the marketing people at the ski resort and asked them about the chances of converting them," Nash says, laughing. "They're still working on that one." ✳

Chapter 4

Becoming A Ski Resort

During the legendary winter of 1983–84, snow fell every day from November 21 to January 2. Here, skiers Don Oakland and Nancy Grey enjoy 40 inches of fresh on Three O'Clock run.

Everyone in Steamboat knew that the arrival of LTV would dramatically alter the future of the valley—they just didn't know how much. Though little actual change occurred at Mt. Werner during the company's inaugural 1969–70 season, by the summer of 1970, LTV Recreational Development had changed the name of the resort to Steamboat Ski Company, unveiled a new logo (the red, white and blue "Steamboat," designed by Dick Hauserman) and developed a 10-year master plan that included a convention center, a base village with underground parking, an eight-story hotel and an 18-hole golf course. The company spent nearly $10 million its first year.

"When LTV bought the ski area, big development came here, and the county hasn't been the same since," says Vernon Summer, who served on Routt County's first planning commission, formed in 1970 largely in response to what was happening on the mountain. "If you'd have told somebody 40 years ago that we'd see a day when there'd be

Below Top: LTV corporate headquarters in Steamboat.
Below Bottom: A list of the company objectives two years after they bought the area.

1973 OBJECTIVES

- SELL ALL COMPLETED CONDOMINIUMS
- SELL REMAINING FAIRWAY MEADOWS LOTS
- MAKE ADDITIONAL RESIDENTIAL LOTS AVAILABLE AND BEGIN SALES
- SELL LAND TO OTHER DEVELOPERS
  - CONDOMINIUM SITES ON KNOLL FOR CONSTRUCTION OF UP TO 250 UNITS IN 1974
  - SINGLE FAMILY ACREAGE, UP TO 300 ACRES
- COMPLETE GOLF COURSE AND BASE I ROADS AND LANDSCAPING
- COMPLETE MASTER PLAN AND ARCHITECTUAL STANDARDS

The six-passenger Bell gondola, built in 1970, had only four towers and included a 3,320-foot span of cable between towers one and two—at the time, the world's longest.

Above: Looking east toward Gondola Square at the beginning of Steamboat's building boom.
Opposite page: Billy Kidd came to work for the Steamboat Ski Company in 1970, six years after winning an Olympic silver medal in Innsbruck, Austria.

10,000 skiers on that mountain, most of them flying in on passenger planes, why you'd have been carted away."

Steve Elkins went to work for LTV in 1970 as "sort of a management trainee," and he got an interesting first assignment: telling the new owners exactly what they'd bought. "My job the first three months was to organize all the property records and tell them what they had—whether it belonged to LTV or whether it'd been sold or whether it was junk or whatever," Elkins says. "I was ready to quit the first week. John Fetcher had all the records in a big box and nothing was put on ledgers or anything—they had check stubs for stuff but no idea what it was for. It was a real education."

Naturally, the sudden appearance of a big company in a small town didn't sit well with everyone. "There were people then, like now, who didn't want anything to change," says Mix Beauvais, who by then had taken over as resort marketing director. "But the business people certainly did, and the people who had kids here were anxious for the resort to take off so that future employment could be created.

And that's proven to be the case in many ways."

From 1970 to 1980, Routt County experienced a growth of nearly 70 percent—to over 10,000 people—with more than half the population in the 18- to 35-year-old age group. "A realtor's dream and a planner's nightmare" is how life-long resident Pete Wither described it in an article for *Steamboat Magazine*. And there was a sense that the growth was almost entirely from skiing, though actually much of it came from another source: coal. Routt County was the top coal-producing county in the state in the late '70s, producing nearly five million tons a year. The power plants that burned it—in Hayden and Craig—paid good salaries and employed almost 2,000 people.

Still, skiing was the industry of the moment. It was what brought LTV into the valley, with the idea of turning Steamboat into a year-round resort. The order had already been placed for the Bell gondola before LTV even arrived, according to Beauvais. "We didn't know how the hell we were going to pay for it," he says, "but we had it ordered." By

After Billy Kidd joined Steamboat in 1970, he posed as Billy the Kid for this promotional photo, wearing cowboy clothes from Hollywood.

the fall of 1970, the gondola was up and running, Olympic silver medalist Billy Kidd had been appointed Director of Skiing and Loris Werner had taken over from his sister Skeeter as director of the ski school.

The hiring of Kidd proved to be a marketing coup that continues to pay dividends for Steamboat over 30 years later. "Billy Kidd is probably the most successful promoter of skiing the sport has ever had," says Glen Paulk, who served as ski area manager from '70 to '74 and as manager and president from '74 to '81. Beauvais recalls the crowds that Kidd would draw on promotional trips to Florida in the mid '70s. "We used to have 400 to 500 people turn out at the Miami Ski Club, just for Steamboat and Billy Kidd," Beauvais says. "In Miami! It was unbelievable."

But while Kidd and his marketing charm were generating interest around the country, the new six-passenger gondola was doing its own promotional work, shuttling guests to the top of Thunderhead at a rate of more than 1,000 skiers an hour. Because there were only four lift towers (as opposed to the 30 that support the current eight-passenger model), the gondola was over 200 feet off the ground in places and included a 3,330-foot span between towers 1 and 2—at the time, the world's longest.

"I spent a lot of time in Europe in the '60s looking at uphill transportation," says John Fetcher, the man primarily responsible for negotiating the gondola's purchase. "At first, they wanted to sell us a system that would bring us to the top of Christie, where we would switch to another system. They didn't have anything that would cover the whole span. But the Bell people had already built a six-passenger one at Mammoth and at Vail, so we knew that's the one we wanted."

All the positive hype the new gondola generated was feared lost on January 23, 1972, when 60-mile-per-hour winds caused a haul cable to rip, sending one of the gondola cars plummeting 150 feet down to the Heavenly Daze run. Luckily, nobody was in the car at the time, and the ensuing investigation found that, had the car been occupied, there would have been enough weight in it to prevent the accident from occurring in the first place. Nevertheless, 140 people had to be evacuated. Ski instructor Irene Nelson, who taught at the resort for 30 years, was working as a hostess in the "Dallas Palace"—what the Steamboat Village Inn was dubbed—the day the car fell.

"The resort, naturally, offered a free meal to everybody

Opposite page: Installing the Priest Creek double chairlift in 1972. It was the first time a helicopter was used at Steamboat to help install a lift. Below: Evacuating one of 140 skiers from the gondola in January 1972. Note the striped ski pants.

The Great Western Freestyle Center

Freestyle skiing competitions were dangerous and unorganized in 1976 and Park Smalley, a former professional competitor, wanted to do something about it. The freestyle scene was sweeping the country, with competitors bringing their much-needed creativity to what they felt was a stodgy and over-regulated sport—too many rules regarding what you could and couldn't do. Yet a slew of injuries during competitions had prevented the sport from being accepted and endorsed by skiing's decision makers. Smalley felt that most of these accidents could be avoided with proper coaching and training facilities and that it was, in fact, the lack of endorsement by the skiing industry that led to many of the problems.

"A few of us had been traveling across the country that summer, putting on freestyle clinics from Squaw to Killington," Smalley recalls. "And after the Killington camp, we were just sitting there having a beer and decided that we should start something ourselves." The other two beer-drinkers were fellow freestylers Rusty Taylor and Mike Williams, both of Steamboat. The threesome decided that Steamboat would be the perfect place to base the camp, so they "jumped in the van, headed west, and by September we were jumping," says Smalley.

Smalley came to the Steamboat Parks and Recreation department and requested permission to construct a training facility at Howelsen Hill. His request was granted and the first "training center"— built later that summer—included two trampolines and a 60-foot polyvinyl snow ramp that tossed jumpers into a pit of straw piled at the bottom. The early days of the center were a bit slow. "There were entire days when I'd just sit there waiting for someone to show up," Smalley remembers,

Top: Park Smalley works with a young GWFC student.
Bottom: Chris Ward, a.k.a. "Neon Deon," showing classic freestyle form.

"and no one did."

Williams was so anxious to check out the ramp that he separated his shoulder by jumping and landing on bare ground. "We needed about 200 bales of hay, and we only had about 80 out there," Smalley says. "But Williams was your typical type-A jumper and was itching to go. So he went down and did a front flip and flew so far out that he cleared the hay entirely—went right over the whole pile and landed on the dirt."

In 1978, the freestyle program was endorsed by the Winter Sports Club, and by the late '70s there was a permanent Great Western Freestyle Training Center (GWFC) at the base of Howelsen, with the team practicing four days a week, including weekends at Mount Werner working on ballet and moguls. The Center had grown to include a water landing called "Rat Lake" (because dead rats were often found floating in it), four trampolines with cool, freestyle-type names like "Air Dog," and a revolving ski carpet where campers could practice ballet moves.

"We started the camps as soon as the snow melted," Smalley says. "And because there were still a lot of injuries happening in the sport, we tried to create a situation where people were taking their crashes in the summertime."

Williams and Taylor moved on after the first year, but Smalley, who later became a driving force behind freestyle skiing's Olympic status, remained head coach at the center and was assisted by his brother, Jon. Together the pair helped train many young competitors on the burgeoning freestyle circuit, and word of the facility spread, bringing many hotdoggers to the Yampa Valley, including six-time U.S. National Mogul Champion and Olympic bronze medalist Nelson Carmichael, who says that some of his best memories are of the annual "More Hair More Air" Tequila Cup, which Mike Williams started in 1974 with his sister, Suzy.

"It was always a pretty crazy event," Carmichael says. "I remember watching pros huck themselves off kickers into the pool, doing all kinds of stuff. Everybody would line the deck, stand up on the roofs, and line up outside to see people coming down the in-run. It was even sponsored by Jose Cuervo at one point."

The GWFC operated from July 1 to September 15. Cooper Schell and Kris "Fuzz" Feddersen, like Carmichael, were early students who went on to successful freestyle careers. Schell first experienced Steamboat as a child on a family ski trip. His family moved to town when he was 11,

and four years later he became a 15-year-old member of the Great Western Freestyle Center squad. He went on to join the U.S. Freestyle Team and was the 1983 U.S. Moguls Champion.

Feddersen participated in the inaugural GWFC summer camp when he was 12 and went on to hold true to the hotdog image, accepting his diploma six years later at the 1982 Steamboat High graduation ceremonies wearing only his graduation cap, boxers, and flip-flops.

The Park Smalley Freestyle Complex was dedicated on December 16, 1999, at Steamboat Ski Resort. It includes the 1,000-foot Voo Doo mogul run and aerial jump facility and was the official training site for the 2002 U.S. Olympic Freestyle Team prior to the 2002 Winter Games. ⨏

A competitor launches large at the annual "More Hair More Air" Tequila Cup, Winter 1983.

involved," Nelson says. "And my son, who was only about 12 or 13 at the time, was one of the people who was stuck on the gondola. Eventually, everybody in the car had to pee, so they drew straws to decide who was going to donate their ski boot."

Three new lifts were added to the resort in 1972, mainly with the goal of reducing lift lines. The first, Christie II, ran to the top of Christie Peak and simply paralleled the original Christie lift. But the other two, the Priest Creek double and the Elkhead double, opened some of the best tree-covered powder stashes in the country: Closet and Shadows.

"It's the one piece the resort was lacking as far as advanced terrain," says Rod Hanna, a former NFL photographer who later became the resort's public relations director. "The only people who were disappointed with that development were the 50 or so locals who'd been going over there for years and had all those tight trees to themselves. There was even an underground trail map to that whole area."

The 1972 season was also marked by Steamboat ski instructor and 10th Mountain Division veteran Rudi Schnackenburg winning the "Ski Instructor of the Year" award from the Rocky Mountain Ski Instructors Association. Schnackenberg, who had previously served as

Above: 10th Mountain Division vet and ski school supervisor Rudi Schnackenburg, was also Howelsen Hill head coach, 1958–60.
Opposite page: Geoff Stump skis the woods in Shadows.

both mountain manager and head coach at Howelsen Hill, had become ski school supervisor in 1967. After he died in 1985, Central Park, a popular trail near the top of the gondola, was renamed Rudi's Run in his honor.

The addition of the Bashor double chair in 1974 opened up a beginner's area above Giggle Gulch, but excitement on the mountain in the early '70s was being generated not by beginners but by "hotdoggers." Wayne Wong was named *SKIING* Magazine's first "Hotdogger of the Year" in 1972, and in 1974, "Concentration," the expert trail below the upper gondola terminal, was designated as the resort's official freestyle trail. "The program is experimental and will remain in effect as long as the hotdog skiers police themselves and use good judgment," said ski instructor Weems Westfeldt, in a January 1974, edition of *Ski Racing* magazine.

With the arrival of the freestyle scene came the party scene. The 1972–73 season saw 1,800 members of the Midwest Collegiate Skiers Association road-trip to town in

> ## "The only people who were disappointed with that development were the 50 or so locals who'd been going over there for years and had all those tight trees to themselves."

over 60 chartered Greyhounds, a trip that was documented by Denver sportswriter Charlie Meyers in a November 1974 *SKI* magazine story entitled "College Blowout." The corn-belt revelers brought 70 kegs along with them, and their weeklong visit culminated with a wet-T-shirt contest at the Village Inn. Rules for the contest stated that contestants "must wear T-shirts or diapers. Or both. Or neither."

The Tugboat Saloon opened on New Year's Eve 1972 and was one of the few watering holes in town at the time. "The ski patrol lived here," says Larry Lamb, one of the bar's original founders. "There was the Buttonbush up the street, and the Dallas Palace, but most people drank here—especially patrol. They would come in here after work, stay until one or two in the morning, then be back again right after work was over [the next afternoon]. You could set your watch by it. The bad thing was, if they had to go find a lost skier on the hill, then they'd all leave and we'd lose our whole customer base."

"I think their ski patrol motto back then was 'get up, go up, show up, and throw up,'" says Hank Edwards, who later became a partner of Lamb's in the Tugboat. "It was on their shirts. Now we're at the point where their kids are coming in. You think that makes us feel old?"

Skier visits at the resort had been steadily climbing every year since 1962, and by the 1975–76 season, they were approaching half a million. Low snow the following year dropped numbers drastically, to less than half that,

The Tugboat Saloon opened on New Year's Eve 1972 and remains a local icon for the beer-swilling set.

Freestyle skiing comps on Mount Werner were a common sight in the mid '70s.

but by 1978 they had surged again, to over 600,000. The area around the mountain was also growing, to match what was being built on the hill. Over two dozen condo projects were completed east of town in the 1970s, and dining and drinking establishments like Dos Amigos, La Montaña and what would later become Mattie Silks and the Inferno all joined the Tugboat on or near Ski Time Square from 1973 to 1979.

With the success of Mount Werner came talk of yet another major ski resort in the valley: Catamount, eight miles away near the base of Rabbit Ears Pass. In fact, a second ski resort, Stagecoach Ski Area, 18 miles south of town, had opened in December 1972, but it closed less than two years later after the owners filed for bankruptcy. (Many skiers considered Stagecoach a real estate development with a few ski runs for enticement, not a serious ski mountain.) There was also Steamboat Lake Ski Area, north of town, which opened in January 1973. But despite being managed by Gordy Wren, its two chairlifts closed down only four months after they opened. Catamount seemed different, with a greater possibility for success because of its size and its close proximity to town. The original development group consisted of a six-man company called Pleasant Valley Investment Corporation, headed by Olympian Marvin Crawford. Plans included construction of over 3,000 housing units, an 18-hole golf course, a 500-acre lake and a new ski resort offering a 3,000-foot continuous vertical drop—proposed as a site for the downhill portions of the proposed 1976 Colorado Winter Olympics.

"I wanted Catamount to happen in the worst way," says Moose Barrows, who had nothing to do with the investment group but cherished the thought of the top-to-bottom descent. "I didn't care about the development, I just wanted it as a skier." First National Bank of Denver ended up owning the 2,863-acre Catamount parcel after a shortage of funds cancelled the project, but not before the developers bought Rehder Ranch and flooded it to create Catamount Lake in 1978. When Northwest Colorado Ski Corporation

bought Steamboat Ski Company in May 1979, they also acquired an option to buy the Catamount land from the bank, thus renewing the debate over adding another ski resort to the valley.

"We had about 265 public hearings on it, not to mention the meetings with all the government agencies," says Steve Elkins, who was also involved with the project and who owns one of the 33 duplexes that help make up the significantly smaller development the project was ultimately reduced to. "It would have been a great ski area."

Denver businessman Martin Hart, who headed the Northwest Colorado Ski Corporation group trying to build Catamount, said one of the main reasons locals were so opposed to another ski area was that they feared major development along the entire eight-mile stretch between them. "And maybe they were right," Hart now says. "I fought hard with the environmentalists at the time—it was a real standoff—but I have family and property in Steamboat and, who knows, it's probably okay that it didn't happen."

The legendary Steamboat Ski School. Irene Nelson (in pigtails) says one instructor—who later became a supervisor—spent an entire winter in the early '70s living in a tent on the mountain with his brother, in between Swinger and Right-of-way runs.

Above: The thin winter of 1976–77 had people shoveling snow onto the runs in order to keep them open.

Opposite page: A conceptual drawing of what would have been Catamount Ski Resort. (The road down from Rabbit Ears Pass is shown in upper left.)

Above top: Not even a snow-calling sacrificial bonfire appeased the snow gods during December of 1976.

Above bottom: The First International Special Olympics helped ease the pain of a dreadfully dry winter.

Meanwhile, Steamboat Ski Area was experiencing its own difficulties. First, Colorado's Olympic bid failed (the state's voters turned it down), and with it the opportunity for Steamboat to host the 1976 cross-country, biathlon and Nordic Combined competitions. Then the winter of 1976–77 turned out to be the worst snow year on record for the resort, forcing closure of the slopes for almost a month. Prior to closure, resort officials instituted a program called "Project Move-It," which involved hauling snow down from Rabbit Ears Pass as well as shoveling it out onto the runs from the trees. Never one to miss a promotional opportunity, public relations director Hanna even had photographers from *The New York Times* come out and take pictures of people hauling truckloads of snow down from Rabbit Ears.

"The whole community got involved however they could," says Loris Werner, who was then director of the ski school. "We at least got a couple trails open to get us

through Christmas." Snow-calling contests and snow-rally sacrificial bonfires were also conducted, aimed at coaxing some of the white stuff from the sky. But despite the best efforts to stave off closure, the slopes shut down on February 13, 1977, and didn't reopen until March 5th.

Poor snow conditions notwithstanding, 1976 also marked the year of one of the most heartwarming events ever to take place on the mountain—the first international Winter Special Olympics. Over 500 Special Olympians were invited to Steamboat to take place in the event, which included appearances by such dignitaries as Oakland Raider Lyle Alzado and Olympic gold medalist Bruce Jenner.

"Everybody in town was broke because there was no snow so there was no work," says Irene Nelson, of the Special Olympics event. "But everyone still participated somehow—I mean even the biggest loadies in the bar were involved. If they didn't do anything else, they were out there

By Sureva Towler

It takes a lot of dope and Dickel to transform a remote frontier town into a world-class ski resort. At Storm Mountain, construction began in the mid '60s, when life was simple, before Lite beer, Tipsy Taxi and flavored condoms. Before the Co-op closed and people began locking their cars and houses. Before the Feds told the county commissioners to stop using old pickups to rip rap the Yampa.

The El Rancho was serving chicken fried steak when developers began designing lifts over cocktails at the Gallery and construction workers arrived to break ground on the mountain's first condo, the Xanadu, and the watering hole called the Buttonbush. The town instantly filled with crazies who wore roach clips, had long hair and put ice cubes in their beer. They skied all day, drank all night and lived on bar snacks. Girls from nice families slept with the guys who took them home when the bars closed, whether they knew their names or not. All hell broke loose.

The lines were clear: You drank red beer or Harvey Wallbangers. You shot elk or did shots. You came from Town or Mountain. You were a Cowboy or a Hippie. You were a Stomp or a Freak. It was easy to distinguish.

Stomps thought hash browns were a vegetable. Freaks ate reinforced brownies. Stomps played pool. Freaks took the 90-meter jump on inner tubes. Stomps stole the Old Man's pickup to poach deer. Freaks zonked on keggers at the Hot Springs. Stomps pulled skijorers down Lincoln Avenue

Top: One thing cowboys and hippies often had in common— a snow-filled mustache. Barry Smith with a face-full.
Bottom: Working on fences wasn't exactly a hippie hobby. Rancher Mike Cannon puts in a day's labor.

during Winter Carnival. Freaks played pinball, smoked dope and lived in beat-up old Volkswagens. Stomps ate Rocky Mountain Oysters at ranch brandings. Freaks held Wet T-Shirt contests at the Cave Inn.

Stomps didn't wear shorts and Freaks didn't chew. If you were a Stomp, the sheriff drove you home when the bars closed. Freaks got arrested for drunk walking. Stomps could become Freaks by smoking pot, but there was no way a Freak could become a Stomp. If your Daddy didn't ranch, you could never become a Stomp. The Sheriff's Department bought two copies of the high school yearbook to create a photo file on possible troublemakers. Youngsters were pulled from cars on Lincoln Avenue and searched for drugs. The sheriff gave one a haircut because "There ain't no Freaks in this town, boy."

The guys building the ski area had Ph.Ds. University professors were fry cooks. Social workers were maids. Lawyers were pumping gas. Debutantes shacked up with hired hands. Mom grew pot and Dad tended bar. Seemingly, everyone had opted out of the life for which education and breeding had prepared them. The caste system was governed by what you did during the day and where you drank at night. You could read 'em by their names: Doper Dan, Gimpy, the Narc, Donna Do (but if you're ugly, Donna Don't). Your profession, rather than politics, religion, heritage or hometown dictated your identity: Chuck the Plumber, Betsy Hairbender, Drywall Bob, Sparky the Electrician. No one had a last name.

A herd of Steamboat hippies shows the sunglasses fashion of the mid '70s.

You could ride a horse into the Inn at Thunderhead, order a drink for yourself and your mount, and both be served. CB radios kept tabs on your kids, your neighbors and the State Patrol. The *Steamboat Pilot's* gossip column and police blotter reported everything anyone needed to know: who got a DUI, who outfoxed the game warden, who got 86'd from the Hatch.

It was common knowledge who blew up the Colorado Bureau of Investigation van housing the narcs, and everyone suspected how the 90-meter jump caught fire. Everyone should have gone to jail: the cowboys who set fire to a kid's hair; the ski area postmistress who put Bloody Marys in mailboxes on Saturday morning; the guys who shot out the bucket rotating above KFC because it blocked their view of the mountain; the crane operator who hoisted a developer's little green Honda to the top of the Ski Time Square sign before leaving town for three weeks. Membership in "The Boots in the Air" and "I Don't Give A Rat's Ass Club" soared.

It was an era marked by working hard and playing hard, hanging out and shooting the shit, pulling capers and doing time. It ended when the sheriff lost the election and real cops started enforcing real laws. Plow jockeys sat elbow-to-elbow at the bar with nail jockeys. Kenny Rogers redefined country music. In Steamboat Springs, the Stomps and the Freaks got tired or grew up, went to jail or died. Some got jobs, married and ran for City Council.

The West has always taken a dim view of the last one over the pass. Indians didn't welcome homesteaders. Cattlemen had no use for sheepmen. No one hung out welcome signs for the men who pushed through railroads, national forests or mines. As the '70s became the '80s, the Good Ol' Boys were equally wary of the quick-buck artists, ski bums, turkeys and Texans who built and occupied 33 condominium complexes between 1979 and 1982. By the time the '80s turned into the '90s, Stomps and Freaks were huddled together down at the VFW complaining about absentee second homeowners, jocks, tree huggers and wealthy newcomers imposing Brie on the land of American cheese. &

Sureva Towler is postmistress at Ski Time Square, 80499, and author of The History of Skiing in Steamboat Springs, *published in 1987.*

shoveling snow out of the woods."

By the following year, LTV was starting to look for potential buyers. Even so, the company still installed the Bar UE and WJW lifts the summer of '77, and brought within the ski area boundary the first truly steep run, Chute One.

"First National Bank mentioned to me that LTV was looking to sell," says Martin Hart, the Denver businessman responsible for organizing a group of Colorado investors who bought the resort in 1979. "And the bank was interested in bringing the ownership back to Colorado." Called the Northwest Colorado Ski Corporation, Hart's group consisted of seven other investors who were ready to make the purchase by the summer of 1977. But first, they had to wait out some ongoing litigation.

Another group called Steamboat Village Resort Corp. (SVRC), headed by Boston businessman Ware Travelstead, was also trying to buy the resort. In fact, Travelstead had been close to buying the resort from LTV the previous year but couldn't come up with the money, claiming that some of his investment group—which supposedly included New York Yankees owner George Steinbrenner—backed out upon learning that Steamboat's gondola was the same make and model as the one involved in an accident in Vail in 1976, in which four people had been killed. In an August 4, 1977, article in the *Steamboat Pilot*, Travelstead's lawyers said that the accident "severely impaired the ability of their client to obtain the financing necessary to complete the sale."

After the Steamboat gondola was certified by the state tramway board, Travelstead said he was ready to pay the $11 million in cash that was due at closing, so he sued to force the sale based on the terms of the original contract.

LTV won the legal battle and ultimately sold the resort to Northwest Colorado Ski Corp. The new owners promptly changed the name to Steamboat Ski Corp., and Hart hired a complete new management team, led by president Hans Geier.

"When I got here, the resort was losing money, and it

Opposite page: Chuck Klesath buried almost up to the pom-pom, 1984.
Below: Early morning on the Bar UE lift, 1979.

Below top: The sparse Steamboat base village in 1979.
Below bottom: Northwest Colorado Ski Corporation leader Martin Hart (left) and Steamboat Ski Corp. president Hans Geier in1986.

Snowmaking became a major part of resort operations in the early '80s, helping save the ski area from a drought in 1980–81, when only 133 inches fell all season. For a time, Steamboat had the most extensive system in the country.

was my job to stop the red ink," says Geier, who served as president of the company for nine years. "LTV was a country club—that's just the way it was run. But Martin Hart was a businessman—he wanted to run it like a ski area."

Shortly after buying the resort, Hart's group sold off several portions of the company, including the golf course and the hotel (to the Sheraton Corp.), reducing the debt almost immediately. Their next big move, prompted by another poor snow year in 1980–81 that dropped skier numbers from above 600,000 the previous season to below 245,000, was to install a $4.2 million snowmaking system. Seventeen miles of air and water lines were installed on the mountain to cover 160 acres of terrain—at the time the most extensive system in the country. It provided a huge boost for Steamboat.

"In the 1970s, we always figured we'd be open by mid December," says Hanna. "But after the snowmaking was installed, we could pretty much guarantee at least some skiing by Thanksgiving, which really helped the local economy."

In addition to snow, another big challenge facing Steamboat at the time was retaining customers. "In the late '70s and early '80s, we were only getting about 40 percent returning skiers," says Geier. "So however many skiers Steamboat was able to get, 60 percent of them had to be new each year—as opposed to Vail, which was getting 80 percent to return, or Aspen, which was getting 90."

Hanna remembers a big part of what changed all that: the "Kids Ski Free" campaign that started in 1982. "It was a major program that really jump-started our numbers and went a long way toward establishing our reputation as a family-friendly ski area," Hanna says. "At the time, the Baby Boomers—who had been a real strong group—were now having kids and were kind of dropping out. So we told them, 'Hey, still come skiing. Just bring your kids and they'll ski free.' We got some of the hotels to let the kids stay free, and we also got the rental shops involved. It worked out really well."

But the biggest move the valley made in terms of growing the ski area was getting the Hayden Airport upgraded and expanded so that jets could fly direct into the Yampa Valley.

Hank Perry had been instrumental in the mid '60s in getting the FAA to invest in a 7,000-foot paved runway in Hayden, but the big jets still weren't flying in. That changed after a joint venture between the resort and the county.

"Getting that crack at the airport expansion was what really made the difference," says Hart. "That's when we started to see real volume coming in." But getting approval from the FAA seemed almost impossible.

"We said to the FAA, 'We want you to extend the runway,' and they said, 'You've got no air service, so we can't do that,'" remembers Hart. "So then we went to American Airlines and got a letter from them saying that they'd fly in if they had the runway. But then the FAA told us we needed existing air service. So that's when we said, 'Okay, tell you what we'll do: We'll build it.'"

And they did. "Commissioner Bill Haight was very instrumental, as were many others in the county," Hart says. "We put a lot into it—well over a million bucks. We just went in there and got the job done."

"Getting the job done" required lengthening the runway from 7,000 feet to 10,500 feet, widening it from 100 to 150 feet, and installing new lighting and an ILS (Instrument Landing System). The original estimate for the work was roughly $4 million, but after the county figured its own labor and equipment into the equation, the cost dropped to less than half that. STOL (Short Takeoff and Landing) aircraft could already fly into Bob Adams airport just two miles northwest of downtown Steamboat, but the decision was made to expand the Yampa Valley Airport instead because there was simply more room for it to grow.

The first flights didn't terminate in Steamboat, and sometimes the business travelers who ended up on those flights were a bit confused when the plane started descending in the middle of the Colorado mountains. "American Airlines had a guy named Mel Olsen who approved all the flights and was in charge of worldwide scheduling," Hart says. "And Mel said he'd help us out by putting us in the guide and listing it as 'Dallas to San Francisco, with one stop.'" We were allowed to sell Dallas–Steamboat—and we sold the hell out of it—but the rest of the people on the plane were these Texas or California business guys who'd gotten a little fare break because of the 'one stop.' Well, you can imagine what they were thinking—they're on their way to San Francisco and all of a sudden they start dropping down in the middle of snow-white country with nothing else around. They thought for sure the plane was crashing."

As the 1970s gave way to the jet age, the community and the resort of Steamboat took stock in the decade it had just left behind. There were growing pains, to be sure: The population had almost doubled from 1974 to 1979. But Steamboat had also become accessible—the one thing most visitors had complained about. By 1986, a skier from Massachusetts could board an American flight in Boston at 6:45 A.M., catch the 9:10 jet out of Chicago, land at the Yampa airport before 11 and be riding up the new gondola by 12:30. Steamboat had hit the big time. ✳

The new runway at Yampa Valley Airport, 1986, equipped to handle big jets. Steamboat Ski Area can be seen in the upper left.

Chapter 5

The Modern Era

Face shots have long been a hallmark of the Steamboat skiing experience.

An expanded airport wasn't the only improvement to usher in the modern era at Steamboat. In addition to direct flights from Chicago, Dallas, L.A. and San Francisco, the mid '80s also marked the arrival of the $4.5 million Doppelmayr eight-passenger Silver Bullet gondola—the first in the world—replacing the 17-year-old six-passenger Bell gondola.

"The Americans [in the ski resort business] used to go to Europe to look at lift equipment," says Hans Geier, then president of Steamboat Ski Corp. "But the Europeans started coming over here to look at our eight-passenger [gondola]." The new gondola had three times the capacity of the old one; load tests were conducted by hauling 763 kegs of Coors Light beer inside the gondola cars. In addition— much to the joy of powderhounds who used to line up early after a storm for a "rope drop" on the upper mountain— a covered, heated 300-person waiting area was added to the bottom terminal, ensuring a more comfortable morning for impatient skiers.

Loading one of the 763 kegs onto the Silver Bullet gondola during testing.

The new eight-passenger gondola instantly tripled uphill capacity at Steamboat.

Also in the mid '80s, several new on-mountain events joined the already popular Cardboard Classic (celebrating its 23rd year in 2003) and Cowboy Downhill (celebrating its 29th year in 2003). For example, in 1986 Steamboat was host to the North American Telemark Championships and the inaugural Jimmie Heuga Express—an event that raised over $25,000 for the United Way. Heuga and Billy Kidd were the first two American men to win Olympic skiing medals. Heuga was later diagnosed with multiple sclerosis; his Jimmie Heuga Express is an ongoing fund-raising effort that involves racers competing for the most vertical feet in eight hours of skiing. Part of what made the 1986 Steamboat event special was that it included competitors Moose Barrows, Loris Werner and Kidd—all members of the 1968 Olympic team.

Also in the fall of '86, the new Valley View trail was finished on the hill creating a major new descent from the top of Thunderhead. And if you were hungry for something other than a cheeseburger, there was now Ragnar's and Hazie's, two fine-dining restaurants located on the mountain. All of these improvements—from big projects like new restaurants and lifts, to smaller changes like sundecks and trail expansion—added immeasurably to the overall idea that Steamboat was gaining ground on the Aspens and Vails of the world. By the end of 1986, Martin Hart's Northwest Colorado Ski Corp. had quietly invested more than $30 million in improvements, and Steamboat had dramatically increased its market share among Colorado ski resorts.

In fact, things were going along so smoothly that change was probably inevitable. "We weren't thinking that much about selling, because we were doing fine and everybody was happy," says Hart. "But at the same time, the ski thing was really moving, and we had been watching the market

Opposite page: By the mid 1980s, the upper gondola building had become a destination unto itself, offering a sundeck, a snack bar and a fine dining experience.
Below: A Stetson-wearing competitor shows his bow-legged form.

Below top: The annual cardboard classic requires creativity and teamwork. But beer helps, too.
Below bottom: The mass-start format of the annual Cowboy Downhill provides plenty of opportunity for humorous mishaps.

The Bump Off

No event in the history of Steamboat skiing combined excitement, inebriation and controversy like the annual Saint Patty's Day Bump Off, which was held on Steamboat's Chute 1 for more than a dozen years. Participants and fans grew from a crowd of about 10 people to over 3,000, until the competition was finally shut down by the U.S. Forest Service, the sheriff's department and the resort in spring of 2002.

Brainchild of a man named Jonny Wisch—proud owner of more than 25 straight Steamboat season passes—the Bump Off began in 1988 ("or somewhere in there," says Wisch. "Those years are a little fuzzy"). It had humble beginnings— simply a small group of guys wanting to test each other on the mountain's meanest run.

"It started as sort of a king-of-the-hill thing," Wisch says. "There were probably seven of us that first year— myself, Chris Ward, Bob Dickey, I can't remember who all was there, but we were just a bunch of guys who used to ski and hang out together."

The annual St. Patty's Day Bump Off drew friendly competitors to the top of Chute 1.

The competition, even in the beginning, used a simple head-to-head format: It started with 16 contestants, and two guys would bomb simultaneously down the chute, with someone judging which one was better. Winners would advance and keep on pairing up until there was only one left standing at the end of the day.

"It was real grassroots back then," says Mike Deimer, who competed in the event starting the second year. "Three guys who didn't want to ski would be the judges— or in Jonny's case, he'd just pick three pretty girls out of the crowd to do it. We'd each throw in 20 bucks, and for that you'd get a T-shirt, about $100 to the winner, and a pair of Hart skis, because Marty Carigan, who was then the local Hart rep, would always throw in a pair of boards."

But as the crowd began to grow each year at the base of Chute 1, so did the problems. "A few guys started to really promote it, and it got huge," says Deimer "People were coming up with tents and kegs and Porta Potties."

By 1999, the resort, now named the Steamboat Ski & Resort Corp., was getting head counts of 2,000 to 3,000 people, and something needed to be done. "Ski area management was getting pretty nervous about it," says then ski patrol director Pete Wither. "So one of the things I tried to do was get my hands around it a little bit and at least get the competitors to sign some sort of liability release. And that worked, but you still had the big crowd at the bottom— which I thought was kind of cool. Yeah, it did get a little out of hand, but everybody sure liked it a lot."

In addition to being a holiday where alcohol usually figured prominently into the equation, revelers at the Bump Off also drank as a way to fend off what were generally cold, miserable conditions. "There were three constants to the Bump Off," Deimer says. "Always Saint Patty's Day, always Chute 1 and always bad weather."

"In defense of Ski Corp., I can understand why they ended it," Deimer says. "People just weren't listening. They started to have these huck-offs on this big jump that they built on the side, and anybody who wanted to could hike up there and go. Then you've got 3,000 drunk people trying to make their way down from the top of the mountain. In the beginning, it was about watching these guys like Bob Dickey, Al Dietrick and Pat Burke—watching them launch some incredible air. That's what made it cooler than just watching your basic bump contest, where it's always twister-spread up top, daffy-twister-spread at the bottom. I wish the Bump Off could've just gone back to the way it was. But, like a lot of things in this town—it ain't gonna." ✦

After a decade of growing popularity, the crowd at the bottom of Chute 1 during the Bump Off competition had swelled to the thousands.

Kimihito Kamori, who bought Steamboat Ski Area in 1989 for $110 million.

the television coverage. He was only going to stay for one day, but he ended up staying four, and before he left we talked about a deal." The eventual sale to Kamori in 1989 netted Hart and his investors $110 million.

"The best ski deal ever" is how Geier describes it. "Hart's group [had] put some money into the ski area, but it was all done with cash flow and small loans—they borrowed less than $10 million. And they kept all the land on the back nine of the golf course, where they're still selling lots."

The idea of Steamboat Ski Area being owned by foreign interests didn't sit well with some of the valley's old-timers, but—with decent capital improvements, a relatively hands-off ownership style and ski visitations topping a million after his first year—Kamori eventually won over most of his critics.

"There was always some grousing about Kamori and frustrations from management about the length of time it took to make decisions," says Rod Hanna, who was then vice president of marketing. "But [Kamori] would eventually make a decision, and it was usually the right one. [He] left us pretty much alone when it came to running the area. We'd have our annual meetings in late April, present the marketing and business plan, and then Kamori would head back to Japan and that was pretty much it. In retrospect, we didn't know how good we had it."

Kimihito Kamori was a skier himself whose company, Kamori Kanko Co. Ltd., had a wide variety of investments

and saw what was paid for Breckenridge, so we were definitely interested."

Breckenridge had been sold in 1988 to a Japanese company called Victoria Company Ltd. for what most people considered a premium price. At the same time, another Japanese businessman, Kimihito Kamori, was looking to invest in a U.S. ski resort. "Kamori owned a ski area in Sapporo [Japan], and he was looking to expand. He wanted to go international," remembers Hart.

Kamori was traveling when the Breckenridge sale took place, and he was disappointed that he'd missed out on the opportunity to bid on it. He wasn't going to make the same mistake again. "Kamori had Salomon Brothers looking at resorts for him, and I had worked with Salomon Brothers before, so that's how we got together," Hart says. "He had been traveling all over looking at ski areas—back East, California, everywhere—so we were just one stop on his big tour. But we had a women's World Cup race going on here at the time, and he was pretty impressed with that—especially

Opposite page: By the early 1990s, snowboarders in the halfpipe were a growing part of the mountain culture.
Below: As word spread of Steamboat's legendary snow, more and more ski bums arrived in town. Some never left their vans.

Nordic Renaissance

By Deb Olsen

Flash and freestyle dominated the glittering world of skiing in the 1980s, while the Nordic Combined discipline went virtually ignored. What kind of sport combines cross-country skiing and jumping, anyway? Crazy. Most Americans thought so, but Steamboat Springs resident Tom Steitz didn't. One athlete at a time, he breathed life into this obscure sport, perhaps knowing that the place that spawned Howelsen Hill in the early 1900s would always have room in its heart for Nordic skiing.

"Nordic Combined skiers share a common outlook," Steitz says. "Throughout the world, they are extremely committed athletes, yet very down-to-earth. There's so much respect among the skiers and coaches that it creates a unique, supportive environment."

When Steitz took over the Steamboat Springs Winter Sports Club Nordic Combined team in 1986, it was basically an after-school activity. What surprised him, however, was that when he moved to the U.S. team in 1988, the outlook wasn't all that different. "Nobody was really ready to reach for the stars," he says. "You make the Olympics, you get that jacket. That was good enough."

Good enough, that is, until Steamboat Springs athlete Ryan Heckman won the U.S. National Nordic Combined Championships in 1991 and boosted the U.S. team to new heights. He and his teammate, Steamboat native Todd Lodwick, registered two U.S. podiums in one year. Ryan

Tim Tetreault, who won three U.S. Nordic Combined titles, in 1992, '93, and '97, and helped lead his team to a tenth place finish at the Nagano Games.

went on to become a two-time Olympian before he retired at the age of 23 to finish college. "Heckman was the one kid who rose to the challenge. He showed the next generation it could be done," Steitz says. "Ryan opened the door, and Todd stepped through it."

What better entrée than when Todd and Ryan posted the first-ever U.S. podium finish in a team event (third place in the two-man sprint) at the debut of the Ski Town USA Nordic Combined World Cup? Although the World Cup events were held downtown, the whole town—with the Steamboat Ski & Resort Corp. at the helm—worked together to make it happen. "The ski area, the city, the people all helped. It was the community that got us there," Steitz says.

Landing a World Cup in its hometown and putting its athletes on the podium moved the U.S. Nordic Combined Team—which by then was headquartered in Steamboat—to a new level. "The whole town was so fired up," Steitz recalls. "Even kids as young as five years old were cheering. Steamboat found its niche."

Someone had the idea to present the winning athletes with gold, silver and bronze cowboy hats instead of the traditional medals. The winners were so taken with them that they wore them throughout the winter. "I remember on the plane going back to Europe, you could look down the aisle and those hats were everywhere," Steitz says. "People would ask, 'Where's Steamboat?' Worldwide, Steamboat has claimed a lot of fame through Nordic Combined."

The team victory was dampened by Lodwick's heartbreak finish in the individual event in the 1995 Steamboat World Cup, when he fell literally at the finish line and dropped from first to third. However, it made his victory the following year even sweeter. Watching Lodwick waving the American flag as he crossed the finish line in 1996 sent the crowd (which consisted of virtually the entire community) to its feet. With Lodwick winning his first gold medal at home, there seemed to be no limit to what the team and Steamboat could do. Unfortunately, one prize continues to dangle just outside of the team's reach: an Olympic medal.

"There's been so many curses on the Big One," Steitz laments. The team headed to the 2002 Games in Park City, Utah hoping to put that curse to rest, but it wasn't to be. The Nordic Combined Team finished fourth, and Lodwick's fifth-place finish in the individual sprint was the highest-ever by an American Nordic Combined skier in the Games. It was still a disappointment to the team, but certainly not to their Steamboat fans, who welcomed them home as heroes. Following the 2002 Games, Steitz announced his retirement. The Nordic Combined renaissance in Steamboat Springs drew to a close on a bittersweet note, as the U.S. Ski Team moved its training grounds to Park City. Steitz looks at it philosophically. "It was an era," he says. "And like all eras, it had to end." ✣

Former reporter Deb Olsen is the editor of Steamboat *magazine and the author of* Steamboat Springs Legends.

Steamboat native Todd Lodwick, who has more than a dozen World Cup podiums and helped lead the Nordic Combined team to a fourth place finish at the 2002 Olympics in Salt Lake.

around the globe—ranging from the huge 4,000-guest Rusutsu Resort outside of Sapporo, Japan, to the Tignes ski resort in the French Alps, to the world's largest koala park, the Lone Pine Koala Sanctuary, in Australia. Kimihito was only 46 years old at the time; it was his father, Katsuo Kamori, then 82, who had built the Kamori Kanko name worldwide.

In addition to bringing new ownership, the start of the '90s delivered a new sport and a new youthful culture to both the mountain and the town: snowboarding. In 1990, shortly after Kamori purchased the resort, the first snowboarding halfpipe was built in Bashor Bowl.

"There was just a super-small group of us at first, maybe a dozen or so riders," says Shannon Dunn, a Steamboat High School graduate who became the first American female to win an Olympic snowboarding medal, taking bronze in Nagano in 1998. "But it didn't take long for kids to start moving here just to board. There was a big crew that came from Southern California and a bunch who moved up from Boulder. It happened pretty fast, but up until I left in '93, you would still get a bunch of snowboarding questions from skiers every time you got on the lift with them."

Though Steamboat was still viewed largely as a family

Above: The ageless snowboarder "Banana" George Blair, still going strong at 87 years young.
Opposite page: Josh Vermette prepares for landing during another fulfilling powder day.

place, the influx of snowboarders did add to the clash between ski bums and cowboys, though not for long. "Now, there's more ski bums than there are cowboys," says Yampa Valley native Pete Wither, who served as Steamboat's ski patrol director throughout the '80s and '90s. "But I don't think it's much of an issue anymore. I think the cowboys decided that everything was going to work out okay—that the skiers and boarders weren't going to try and take their land or whatever." Today, snowboarders can make up as many as half of all people at the resort on any given day.

Not only was there an influx of youthful snowboarders: Steamboat also became home to a snowboarding legend. Sherman Poppen—one of the sport's founding fathers—moved to Steamboat in the early 1990s. Back in 1965, Poppen had invented a surfing-on-snow device he called the "Snurfer" by screwing together two children's skis for his daughter, Wendy. Less than a year later, he licensed the

> "There was just a super-small group of us at first, maybe a dozen or so riders, but it didn't take long for kids to start moving here just to board."

Above: More than 200 inches of snow fell in January alone during the colossal winter of 1996–97.
Opposite page: Eric Bergoust flies high over Voo Doo, in the Steamboat Bumps and Jumps competition.

Snurfer idea to the Brunswick Corp. Close to a million Snurfers were sold over the next 10 years. The Snurfer was the precursor to the modern snowboard—existing 10 years before Dimitrije Milovich started selling his Winterstick boards and 12 years before Jake Burton Carpenter and Tom Sims started selling theirs. Poppen, dubbed the Grandfather of Snowboarding, is now an honorary instructor for the resort's snowboard school and will sometimes drop in on a class, much to the delight of students.

Poppen wasn't the only retiree to settle in Steamboat at an age when many are considering a move to Arizona or Florida. War hero Robin Olds—a retired Air Force fighter pilot with 19 aerial victories and 900 hours of combat in both World War II and Vietnam—moved to town in 1973 and has continued to ski every year since. As has 87-year-old "Banana" George Blair, a tireless self-promoter who was born in Toledo, Ohio, in 1915 and learned to snowboard at the age of 75. Blair still spends much of his winters in Steamboat and can often be seen swooping down the slopes of Mount Werner in his bright yellow suit.

Freestyle skiing has also experienced a huge resurgence at Steamboat in recent years. By 1998, Steamboat had hosted the annual Bumps and Jumps competition, a televised pro-am event that has drawn the likes of Olympic gold medalists Eric Bergoust and Jonny Moseley. The hosting of Bumps and Jumps also helped cement Steamboat's reputation as a leader in the emerging pipe-and-park movement, as did the addition of the Mavericks Superpipe in Bashor Bowl. At over 600 feet, it was the longest in North America in the 2001–02 season.

The Sunshine Reef Terrain Park opened in 1996—which turned out to be a good year for soft landings. Steamboat received almost 450 inches of snow in 1996–97. The season surpassed even the legendary winter of 1983–84, when it began dumping on November 21 and didn't stop for a month and a half. That season was one of five that Ben Tiffany spent as a lift operator at the resort, making him one of the few people in town to experience both epic snow years in all their glory.

"It was the best December of skiing I've ever had," Tiffany says of the storm in '83. "A lot of people were out there every morning at first, but after a couple of weeks, everybody was worn out, and there were only about a half dozen of us each morning."

Outdoor Gear Manufacturers Call Steamboat Home

It should come as no surprise that the creativity so often fostered in the mountains has manifested itself in the form of several small but successful outdoor-based manufacturers in Steamboat.

While all these companies and entrepreneurs have displayed a high level of creative ambition, none can yet claim the longevity or, perhaps, the level of innovation shown by Kent Eriksen, who arrived in Steamboat from Wisconsin on his bike on December 31, 1974.

"It was 44 below zero," Eriksen remembers. "But I was just too broke to go any further." Steamboat's mountain biking community should be forever grateful.

Though Eriksen's first job was in a photo lab, he opened the Sore Saddle Cyclery in the summer of 1975, leasing space in the back of a local ski shop. He didn't have much competition. "There was really no other bike shop in town at the time," he says. "Some German guy over by Fairview used to operate out of his house, but that was about it."

Eriksen ran the Sore Saddle for five years, during which time he began experimenting with some of his own frame designs. He also became very involved in promoting the sport of biking locally, including organizing the first Tour de Steamboat in the summer of 1975. By 1980 he had purchased a small piece of property at the west end of town, next to the park at 12th and Yampa. He'd also found the perfect building to put there—a 40-foot high metal tepee.

"I bought it from the city, who'd used it to burn wood chips," Eriksen says. "It was pretty unconventional, but there were no architectural restrictions at the time so I wrapped it in chicken wire and ferro-cement and that became my shop." A small dairy building was attached later

Top: Mountain Bike Hall of Fame member Kent Eriksen, an innovator of titanium bike frames.
Bottom: Peter and Patricia Duke, founders of SmartWool—a popular outdoor apparel company.

on, a structure that now serves as Sore Saddle's service center.

Eriksen went to bike-frame school in Oregon in 1980 and by the following year he'd created the Moots Mountaineer—a classic steel-frame bike. (The name Moots comes from a small plastic alligator that Eriksen had stuck on the end of his pencil in third grade.)

In 1991, Eriksen started building bikes from titanium instead of traditional steel, a move that set the Moots brand apart for its light weight and durability. "They were by far the lightest bikes available at the time," Eriksen says.

By 2001, Moots had outgrown its old facility and moved its headquarters to a 15,000-square-foot warehouse that included attached employee housing. The company currently produces almost 1,000 bike frames a year. (Only about 10 percent of Moots bikes go out fully equipped; most are just frames that are shipped to dealers.)

Though Eriksen, who was inducted into the Mountain Bike Hall of Fame in 1996, sold his ownership in Moots, he remains active in the company. "I still design and build the bikes—all the blue-collar stuff," Eriksen says. "Which is what I'm best at anyway."

Another entrepreneur, Ed Watson, moved to Colorado in 1993 and started Fat Eddy's Threadworks while living near Estes Park, one of the gateways to nearby Rocky Mountain National Park. Originally from Nashville, Watson sat down at his mother's sewing machine in Tennessee and started creating gear to satisfy his caving and climbing habits.

"I went out on the road with it at first, selling accessories like watch bands, chalk bags, bivy sacks, that sort of thing," Watson says. "But nobody wanted to build me a shop

Kent Eriksen moved to town in 1974 and opened one of the first bike shops in town—the Sore Saddle.

so I found one up in Steamboat."

Watson took on a couple partners and moved his sewing machines into a warehouse in west Steamboat in 1997. The company continued making climbing gear, but branched out into paddling accessories in 2000. Fat Eddy's continues making a variety of outdoor products and he and partner John Cardillo recently started a new company aimed at canine customers. Look for the Spiffy Dog brand on a pooch near you.

Like Fat Eddy's, Bill Gamber's BAP! technical clothing company (as well as two other companies he co-founded, Big Agnes sleeping bags and Stinger energy goo) was inspired at least in part by his desire to satisfy his own outdoor pursuits. Gamber—a climber, fisherman and successful triathlete—arrived in Steamboat in 1991 with more skis than money, but has since built a respected retail and manufacturing business right in the heart of downtown.

"I basically just sit here in my office looking out at Buff Pass, wishing I was up there instead," says Gamber. "And the view has generated a lot of ideas about building

One of the most basic pieces of "gear" for the outdoors, of course, are the socks you put on your feet. And sock lovers everywhere are becoming familiar with the name SmartWool, which has grown in popularity ever since founder Peter Duke first introduced it at a Las Vegas trade show in 1994. Duke was already living and working in town, teaching skiing at Steamboat Ski Resort while peddling his woolen wares out of the back of his car. Duke's company now employs about 35 people in town and has done nothing short of create a rebirth of wool, adding underwear, gloves, gaiters and other items to its already strong brand of socks (though socks remain 90 percent of the company's business).

Even Olympian Nelson Carmichael started a local outerwear company—1080 Degrees—aimed at making functional snow apparel that appeals to snowboarders, skiers and telemarkers alike. Carmichael introduced a product line in the fall of 2001 that includes jackets, pants and accessories.

"The goal is to offer quality clothing regardless of what sport people participate in," Carmichael says. "We hope ou

As for the 1996–97 season, when the resort set a record for the month of January (216.5 inches), Tiffany says at times it seemed there was too much snow. "It was almost overwhelming, especially on the roads," he says. "People were driving around with flags tied to the tops of their antennas, because you couldn't see around the corners."

The timing of the '96–'97 storms coincided nicely with the addition of the new Morningside Park—a 179-acre expansion on the back side of Storm Peak that included the steepest inbound runs on the mountain and a lift bringing skiers right to the top of Chutes 1, 2 and 3. But the new lift wasn't welcomed by everyone.

"There are still a couple guys who have never ridden that lift," says local skier Dan Gilchrist. "And Ben Tiffany is one of them. Peter Ashek's the other. They'll just hike up from Storm [Peak], and they'll beat you to the top every time." Tiffany is one of Steamboat's last great ski bums, along with the likes of Jim Mader and longtime resort night janitor Steve Myers—guys who continue living the dream that so many start but so few continue. "Ben's gone into work at Dos Amigos at four o'clock every day for 15 years," says Gilchrist. "All he does is cook, and he skis every single day of every single season. They've tried to move him up on the line, but he doesn't want the responsibility or the stress. He wants to ski."

Gilchrist is no stranger to the ski-bum life himself. Though he now has a day job, he moved to town in 1986 and

Opposite page: Dan Gilchrist, rock-hopping in the Steamboat backcountry. Below: Dan Gilchrist, smiling through evidence of another powder day.

Ben Tiffany displays the mementos from more than 20 years of a dedicated ski bum lifestyle.

continues to make a name for himself as a frequent telemark skier in the annual Warren Miller ski movie. He began making turns for cinematographer Chris Patterson shortly after both of them moved to town, and if snow conditions on the mountain don't cooperate (a rare occurrence), Gilchrist will sometimes guide the film crew to ample stashes in the backcountry, either off the back side of the resort or on nearby Buffalo Pass. "That's a big part of the reason why I've never left here," Gilchrist says of the Steamboat backcountry. "You don't hear much about it, but it consistently has the best and deepest snow."

Not that good snow on Mount Werner is ever too difficult to find. By the late 1990s, as Steamboat's inbounds terrain pushed closer and closer to 3,000 acres, the resort continued to receive the best powder in Colorado, rivaling the legendary dumps at Alta, Utah. "Sitting at 10,000 feet and being 1,000 miles from the ocean simply makes for the perfect combination," says Billy Kidd, who has likely skied more places around

Downtown Steamboat at dusk reflects both the ski mystique and the cowboy culture that make up the town.

the world than anybody else in town. "The Andes, the Southern Alps, the Sierra—they all get a lot of snow, but it's just not as fluffy as here."

And on that rare occasion when skiers and snowboarders can't find powder on the mountain, not even in the "secret" spots, there is another option just west of the ski area. Jupiter and Barbara Jones opened Steamboat Powder Cats on nearby Buffalo Pass in 1983, and the operation—now owned by Blue Sky West—provides access to more than 15 square miles of bountiful face shots. Though most of the slopes are moderately angled, the company recently added some advanced terrain in the Soda Creek drainage that will please those seeking steeper slopes.

In the summer of 1997—after the project had been post-poned for two years—the Arrowhead triple chair and Thunderhead double chair were both removed and replaced with the Thunderhead Express high-speed quad. The new detachable lift was part of a $3 million project that, along

with the first phase of the Pioneer Ridge expansion, proved to be the last major capital improvement for Kamori. The following fall, in early November 1997, the American Skiing Company (ASC), then headed by entrepreneur Les Otten, announced that it had completed the purchase of both Steamboat and Heavenly at Lake Tahoe, California, from Kamori for the combined price of $288.3 million.

Steamboat and Heavenly marked the eighth and ninth resorts for ASC, which already owned Sunday River and Sugarloaf in Maine, Attitash Bear Peak in New Hampshire, Killington, Mount Snow and Sugarbush in Vermont, and The Canyons in Utah. The company had previously raised over $265 million through an initial public offering of its stock, which was offered at $18.

The first year went pretty smoothly for Steamboat's new owners, with the company promoting a few local employees to higher positions within ASC. During the summer of 1998, the Pony Express high-speed quad was added to service a dozen new trails in the Pioneer Ridge area, and in September, Olympic gold medalist Jonny Moseley signed on with ASC as a sponsored athlete. Two months later, on November 6, 1998, Les Otten was honored by being asked to ring the closing bell that ends the trading day on the New York Stock Exchange.

But the following year, in the spring of 1999, the company let go several high-profile longtime locals, including 30-year employee Pete Wither. The move created a firestorm of local resentment toward the new owners, as evidenced by the proliferation of bumper stickers bearing slogans like "MORE FOR LES, LESS FOR STEAMBOAT," "MORE STEAMBOAT, LESS OTTEN," and "WHY, FOR PETE'S SAKE?"

"There was a huge clash," says Rod Hanna, who retired in the summer of 2000. "The company showed no sensitivity to the local way of doing things."

"Unless you recognize and integrate the local heritage into your program, then there's no way you're going to be successful," adds Moose Barrows. "That's where Les Otten got into trouble—he didn't learn the heritage of the place, so he couldn't make use of it."

On March 28, 2001, Les Otten resigned from ASC—the stock price had fallen to less than $1—and was replaced by new CEO William J. Fair. Almost exactly one year later, ASC was set to sell Steamboat for $91.4 million to a group of investors called Triple Peaks, headed by Vermont residents Tim and Diane Mueller, owners of Okemo Mountain Resort in Vermont. (The Muellers had also been two of the purchasers of the Catamount area six years earlier.) The deal with the Muellers ultimately fell through when ASC sold its Heavenly ski area to Vail Resorts instead. Shortly thereafter, ASC moved its company headquarters from Maine to Park City, Utah, to be closer to its two big Western resorts, Steamboat and The Canyons.

ASC seems well aware that it owns one of the jewels of the ski industry. After 40 years, the mountain consists of 142 trails spread out over nearly 3,000 acres. The ski school has over 400 instructors, continually sharing the mountain and the sport with thousands of visitors every year, some new, some who've been coming for years. And of course, perhaps even most important, Mount Werner continues to average over 300 inches of snow each winter.

Like so many mountain towns, Steamboat struggles with growth, with the inevitable lack of affordable housing, with the notion that some members of the still-small community live below the poverty line while others can afford a private helipad. "I can remember when people would give someone a bad time because he'd paid $12,000 for a house downtown," says realtor and lifelong resident Steve Elkins. "I can hardly believe it myself." The average price of a single-family home in the Yampa Valley in August 2001 was $835,891.

But people pay for quality, and in Steamboat, quality is what they get. Quality neighbors, quality sports, quality of life. And of course, quality snow. It's the one constant in an ever-changing community. Many uncertainties will surely make the next 40 years on Mount Werner as exciting and unpredictable as the last. There may be different owners, there will certainly be different skiers and more snowboarders, and there will likely be different Olympians. But the snow will still fall, and Steamboat will remain Ski Town USA. ✷

Routt County tradition—a cowboy, his truck and his dog.

Chapter 6

Competition

Like many before him, 14-year-old Steamboat local Graham
Hogrefe aspires to become an Olympian.

"There are two places you can finish in a race," Wallace "Buddy" Werner once said. "And I only want one of them."

Werner's will to win, a desire seemingly planted in every Steamboat skier at birth, has guided hundreds of boys and girls, men and women, from starting gate to finish line to podium. But while Werner may have best exemplified the competitive spirit of Steamboat (as a high school quarterback, he once hid his broken nose from the coach so he wouldn't have to come out of the game), he was certainly not the only ski star to rise from the Yampa Valley.

The residents of Steamboat have shown throughout the years that they don't care whether the prize is a trip to the Olympics, a trophy, a pair of goggles or a pat on the back—they just like to compete. They will race uphill, downhill, across a meadow or down the middle of Main Street being pulled by a horse.

The first competitive ski event in Steamboat was likely

The face of competition: Olympian Buddy Werner for whom Mount Werner and Buddy's Run are named.

Phil Guthrey (on horse) pulls a young skijorer down Steamboat's Lincoln Ave. Winter Carnival, 1932.

The first Winter Carnival, Woodchuck Hill, 1914. This is the present site of Colorado Mountain College.

the jumping competition at the 1914 winter carnival, which included a dozen young boys launching themselves off the jump on Woodchuck Hill. Ten years later, two Steamboat men, Louis Dalpes and Covert Hopkins, represented Colorado at tryouts for the first Olympic Winter Games, to be held in Chamonix, France. Though neither of them qualified, Dalpes did become Colorado's first state jumping champion the following year.

In 1932, 24-year-old John Steele, a local jumper who had been coached by Carl Howelsen and who had won the Rocky Mountain Jumping Championships at Howelsen Hill in 1929 and 1930, became Steamboat's first Olympian. Two other Steamboat men—Dalpes and Glen Armstrong—also tried out in '32, but Steele was the only one to qualify. He competed in the ski jumping events at Lake Placid, New York, finishing 15th out of 35 jumpers.

Cross-country ski racing was a large part of the annual winter carnival, and the list of early winners shows the versatility of many Steamboat skiers from that era. Carl Howelsen himself won the carnival's cross-country event in 1915 and 1916, and Bill Dalpes—Louis' brother—won it in 1922. Tenth Mountain Division veteran Gordy Wren won the carnival's cross-country race both before (1943) and after (1949) his participation in World War II.

Alpine racing didn't make its appearance in Steamboat until the 1930s. In fact, it wasn't until 1931, when the Denver and Rio Grande Railroad hired a man named Graeme McGowan to come and teach the people of Steamboat a new turn called the Kristiania that the sport of "slolom" (the spelling the *Steamboat Pilot*—the local paper—initially gave it) started to take hold. Even then, most of the young students only took McGowan's classes because it meant getting out of school early.

Unfortunately for McGowan, 1931 was a horrible snow year, and though his Steamboat students were excited about the new "crouching" turn, there wasn't enough snow to hold a race. As Jean Wren wrote in her book, *Steamboat Springs and the Treacherous and Speedy Skee*, "the racing would have to wait…In the meantime, everyone would have to remember 'how that turn thing went.'"

The new sport finally made its debut in the form of a 110-yard slalom down the east face of Howelsen Hill at the winter carnival of 1933, but it wasn't until 1935 that the town's skiers really embraced the concept. That's the year the Steamboat Springs Winter Sports Club hired a man

Glen Armstrong, (below) tried out for the 1932 Olympic team with Steamboat's first representative to the Games, John Steele.

Howelsen Hill, 1932. Though slalom races were starting to appear around the country by the early 1930s, jumping remained the focus in Steamboat.

named Bob Balch to come up from Denver for an entire month and give group lessons to the club.

Even after Balch's arrival, jumping events and cross-country races remained the competitions that really fired up Steamboat skiers. According to Sureva Towler's *History of Skiing at Steamboat Springs*, Gordy Wren, in an act of defiance during an early slalom race at Berthoud Pass, was disqualified when he threw his poles away after crossing the finish line with the fastest time.

"The first time I ever saw a guy turn was when I was 13 or 14 when Junior Duncan from Estes Park came over to the ski carnival," Wren said in a December 1968 article in *SKIING* Magazine. "I said to myself, 'Look at that sissy, what's he doing? That's no way to ski.' Up to that time, I hadn't ever made a turn except at the bottom of the jumping hill."

In February 1939, the first official down-mountain race took place in Routt County. It was won by Horace Button, who traveled over from Hot Sulphur Springs and competed on the first Groswold skis to be built with metal edges. Five

years later, in 1944, the Winter Sports Club hired Al Wegeman to coach the town kids.

"He was like the Pied Piper," says Marvin Crawford, an early student of Wegeman's and one of seven skiers Wegeman helped prepare for Olympic competition. "We'd ski to school, and then we'd all follow him over to Howelsen Hill to ski and race under the lights after dinner."

Shortly after Wegeman's arrival, his ski lessons were recognized as an official part of the learning program for kids—giving Steamboat the honor of becoming the first school district in the nation to make skiing an accredited part of the school curriculum. The cost of Wegeman's salary was divided between the school district and the Winter Sports Club, and though enrollment was optional, three-fourths of eligible school kids signed up for his classes.

Five of the six members of the 1954 U.S. Ski Team were Wegeman students: Crawford, Skeeter and Buddy Werner, Katy Rodolph and Wegeman's son, Keith (Wegeman's older son, Paul, had been on the U.S. Nordic Combined team at the

The Winter Sports Club

By Tom Ross

On a typical Rocky Mountain Wednesday night in February, when families elsewhere are balancing homework with TV sitcoms, a sizeable portion of the children of Steamboat Springs can be found hefting improbably long skis over their shoulders and propping them against the log walls of a ski lodge that evokes another era.

Trooping into the Howelsen Hill Lodge, the skiers clap the snow off their bodies and squeeze into spots on heavy wooden benches, mindless of the ski greats who have occupied those same benches before them. There is even a sprinkling of 30-somethings, looking even more excited than the nine-year-olds. They've all got one thing in mind—flying through the air.

On Wednesday nights in Ski Town USA, it's come one, come all, to the Hitchens Brothers Wednesday Night Ski Jumping Series. It's a tradition in this town of about 10,000 that is maintained by the oldest ski club west of the Mississippi—the Steamboat Springs Winter Sports Club.

"It's an amazing thing when I think back and recall that adrenaline rush when you're eight years old and you're about to go off a 50-meter ski jump," says Scott Wither.

Wither, 30, is emblematic of the unquenchable enthusiasm for ski competition that wells out of Howelsen Hill like water from one of the town's 105 springs. A former U.S. Ski Team alpine competitor and a national slalom champion for the University of Colorado, Wither had launched a successful career in information technology when he heard Howelsen Hill calling him back. Today, Wither helps coach 56 young ski racers 9 to 12 years old, all members of the Winter Sports Club, training on the same hill where their coach grew up. It has been like this for decades in Steamboat—each succeeding generation passing it forward.

The club isn't limited to ski jumping. It has openly

Bob Wither, dubbed "The Boy Wonder" in 1925 after jumping 85 feet as a nine-year-old.

embraced every discipline of snow sport, and its professional staff actively encourages children to move from alpine to snowboarding, or from Nordic Combined to freestyle, if that's what's in their hearts.

Wither was destined to become a slalom racer, but there has always been a Nordic skier inside him. He relishes the story of how his grandfather, Robert Wither, was known in Steamboat as "The Boy Wonder" after he jumped the 90-meter ski jump as a nine-year-old. Scott himself jumped the 70-meter as an 11-year-old with his father, Pete.

"It was just something we'd always done," Wither says. "We were just trying to get more air."

Today, the Steamboat Springs Winter Sports Club is one of the few institutions that keeps the jumping tradition alive, training young and old alike in the art of flying on skis. The growing enrollment has topped 600, and Sarah Floyd, the club's athletic director, holds the conviction that it is the unpretentious log lodge with its giant fireplace and homey concession stand that first gets a grip on people in Steamboat.

"It's what many of us grew up with as skiers," Floyd says. "The old lodge, the fireplace, the hot dogs and hot chocolate. Nothing is locked up—everyone's gear is stuffed under the wooden tables."

It's at Howelsen Hill that the Winter Sports Club trains not only future World Cup and Olympic ski jumpers, but Olympic slalom and downhill racers, freestyle mogul skiers, snowboarders, cross-country skiers and Nordic Combined athletes. Over the years, 54 Winter Olympians have trained with the club, including 17 that went to the 2002 Winter Olympics in Salt Lake. Some came to Steamboat for two years of work that catapulted them onto the national team; others grew up in the Yampa Valley, taking part in Wednesday night ski jumping.

In Wither's group of 50-plus ski racers, there is almost certainly a Junior Olympic champion waiting to happen. And maybe even a talent who will ski on the World Cup as Wither did.

"We set goals each year, and it's not a ludicrous thought for one of these kids to say, 'I'm going to be an Olympian,'" Wither says. "It's a realistic goal when you find yourself training on a Tuesday night with a guy who just came back from the World Cup."

Across its different disciplines, the club's coaching staff is sprinkled with skiers who have taken part in World Championships and Winter Olympic Games. The kids just know them as Heidi and Todd and Gary and Nelson. Of course, it would be a disservice to portray the Steamboat Springs Winter Sports Club as an organization with the sole mission of producing Olympic skiers. For most of its athletes, the benefits will include acquiring lifetime skills,

an unshakable work ethic and the self-reliance that comes from traveling the nation and the world to compete.

Still, it's hard to ignore all of those flags hanging from the rafters in Olympian Hall on the second floor of Howelsen Hill Lodge. The room is where families gather for potluck suppers at the beginning and end of each ski season. There is a flag for each club member who became an Olympian, reflecting the country where he or she competed in the Winter Games. It's a silent reminder that in Ski Town USA, dreams of Olympic proportions really do come true. ⑤

Tom Ross is a reporter and photographer for the Steamboat Pilot *who has been covering sports in the valley for more than 20 years.*

Top-notch teaching and coaching has been a Winter Sports Club tradition for decades.

Oslo Olympics of 1952). "He gave us all the basics," Skeeter Werner said of Wegeman in Smokey Vandergrift's *Steamboat Centennial* video. "He was a wonderful teacher."

Wegeman was also one of the first people in the valley to suggest that skiing be developed on Storm Mountain. He left Steamboat in 1949 to teach skiing at Sun Valley, Idaho, and he died of cancer the following year. Though many in town were sad to see Wegeman leave, his departure opened the door for the return of Gordy Wren, one the Yampa Valley's favorite sons and fiercest competitors.

Wren was a third generation Steamboat native, born in 1919. He taught skiing at Alta, Utah (1941–42), and Winter Park, Colorado (1945–47), prior to being selected for the 1948 U.S. Olympic team. In between, he served as an instructor for the famed 10th Mountain Division and as the University of Denver's first ski coach. While training for the Olympics in Aspen, he met a young reporter for the *Aspen Times* named Jean Maxwell, and they were married later that year.

Wren was first inspired to become an Olympian after John Steele spoke at a school assembly when Wren was in eighth grade. Many years later, fresh from his 1948 Olympic appearance in St. Moritz, Switzerland, Wren was eager to pass on the knowledge gleaned from the experience. During the following six years, from 1949 to 1955, he would coach, teach or assist in teaching an astounding 12 Olympians: all three Werner kids, Marvin Crawford, Moose Barrows, Jere and Jon Elliot, Paul and Keith Wegeman, Crosby Perry-Smith, Ted Farwell and Katy Rodolph.

Rodolph (later Rodolph-Wyatt) went on to win nine U.S. National Championships, before breaking her neck at the last women's race ever held on the famed Hahnenkamm downhill course at Kitzbühel, Austria. She was briefly married to fellow Olympian Paul Wegeman, who joined his younger brother, Keith, on Willy Schaeffler's championship University of Denver team from 1949 to 1951.

"He just did something to people," Skeeter Werner said of Wren in *Steamboat Centennial*. "Gordy has to be credited

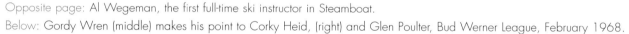

Opposite page: Al Wegeman, the first full-time ski instructor in Steamboat.
Below: Gordy Wren (middle) makes his point to Corky Heid, (right) and Glen Poulter, Bud Werner League, February 1968.

with making this Ski Town USA."

Skeeter, of course, was Gladys Werner, a member of the triumvirate of Olympic power known collectively as the Werner kids. The Yampa Valley has been home to many great families with competitive siblings: Ray, Delbert and Corky Heid; Jon and Jere Elliott; Mike and Suzy Williams; Jace, Lance and Brent Romick; Moose and Nancy Barrows, all six Bowers children; and Keith, Paul, Laurie and Dorothy Wegeman. But none of them have left the mark of the three Werners.

"[Our parents'] overall attitude toward work was what really built the foundation for us," says Loris Werner of his parents, Hazie and Ed "Pop" Werner. "But they did more than just make us work hard. They were demanding but also supportive in whatever we wanted to do. I don't remember either of them ever interfering with any decision made by a coach, no matter what the reason."

After watching her kids ski for so many years, Hazie herself picked up skiing—when she was 65. "And she skied right up to the end," Loris says. "She was 82 when she died, and she was still at it." Hazie had come from a true pioneer family. Her father had been a stagecoach driver on the run between Wolcott and Hahns Peak before Steamboat had railroad service.

Loris, the youngest of the three Werner children, competed in the Junior National Championships for four years,

from 1955 to 1958, winning both the downhill and jumping titles his final season. He was a member of the U.S. Ski Team for nine seasons, from 1959 to 1968, and won the downhill in the U.S. National Alpine Championships in 1967.

"Me and Buddy, we spent most of our winter nights downstairs messing around with our skis," Loris says. "We were always trying to make them a little faster, always trying to figure out a way to get a little better edge on somebody."

Loris made two Olympic teams and went on to play an active role in many aspects of skiing in Steamboat. He became the Steamboat Springs Winter Sports Club/Howelsen Hill head coach in 1968–69, taking over from his sister, Skeeter, and he returned for a second stint at Howelsen in 1972–73. He has spent over 30 years working at the Steamboat ski resort, serving as everything from ski school director to operations manager. It was Loris who designed and helped build the downhill courses for the first-ever World Cup races in Steamboat, in February 1989 and December 1990.

Opposite page: Buddy Werner with his mom, Hazie, and father, Ed, known to everyone in town as "Pop."
Below: Katy Rodolph, slalom, giant slalom and downhill racer, was a member of the 1952 and 1956 Olympic teams.

Like her two younger brothers, Skeeter Werner came to prominence as an outstanding junior competitor, winning both the slalom and downhill at the U.S. Junior National Alpine Championships in 1948. And, like brother Loris, she had a knack for teaching others, coaching for both the Colorado Junior Nationals team and the Steamboat Springs Winter Sports Club before founding Steamboat's ski school in 1962, 10 years after being selected to her first Olympic team.

At the 1956 Olympics in Cortina d'Ampezzo, Italy, Skeeter was the top American, placing 10th in the downhill. She went on to a successful career in fashion, working as both a designer and model in New York and around the world. In 1955, Skeeter and football great Doak Walker appeared on different covers of *Sports Illustrated*. Fourteen years later they were married. They lived in Steamboat for many years. Doak died in the fall of 1998, and Skeeter passed away on July 20, 2001, after a long battle with cancer.

As for Buddy Werner, it is difficult to describe a man so many loved and admired. He remains, nearly 40 years after his death, an emotional and spiritual leader in the town that produced him.

Buddy's great career began when he won the slalom and downhill at the Junior Nationals in 1952. He was named to the U.S. Ski Team two years later and became the first American to win a major European downhill event when he

Above: Like all three Werner kids, Skeeter was a fierce competitor. Opposite page: Loris Werner racing; as Buddy (right) looks on. Chuck Leckenby, editor of the *Steamboat Pilot*, reaches for his camera.

beat Austria's mighty Martin Strolz at the Holmemkollen in February 1954. Even bigger than the Holmemkollen victory was the win four years later when Buddy beat the seemingly invincible Austrian Toni Sailer by over two seconds in the Hahnenkamm downhill.

"Until Buddy came along, we had no idea we could beat the Europeans," says fellow Olympian Moose Barrows. "He was the one who made us all believe we could do it."

Buddy was the U.S. national alpine champion in '57 and again in '59—the same year he was voted the National Ski Association's Skier of the Year. He made three Olympic teams: 1956, 1960 and 1964, but hard luck seemed to hound him. At the '56 Games he lost skis in two of his races (though he still managed to place 11th in the downhill, finishing the race on one ski). Just before the 1960 Olympics at Squaw Valley, California, where he was a favorite to win a medal, he broke his left leg while training at Aspen.

After his accident, in the February 1960 issue of *SKI*

> "Until Buddy came along, we had no idea we could beat the Europeans. He was the one who made us all believe we could do it."

The Winter Carnival

Many small towns across America take pride in hosting annual celebrations of one type or another, but it would be difficult to find a homegrown festival anywhere in the country that matches the tradition and spirit of the Steamboat Springs Winter Carnival, which has taken place the second week of February for nearly 90 years.

No surprise that it was Carl Howelsen who played the leading role in creating the first carnival in 1914, replanting the midwinter community celebration halfway around the globe from his native Norway, where similar events had been held for years. But while Howelsen may have organized the first one, the winter carnival has grown through the years because it's been nurtured, cultivated and cared for by literally thousands of Steamboat volunteers—from school kids to Olympians to grandparents.

Though the jumping events were certainly the most popular aspect of that first carnival, they were far from the only activity. Other competitions included a 10-mile cross-country race (in which Carl Howelsen placed second, a testament to his well-rounded skiing skills), a shooting match and a "ladies' free-for-all" race, where women competed in traditional winter outfits, including long wool skirts.

The second winter carnival saw the introduction of skijoring, an event whose popularity would grow to rival even that of ski jumping and would become one of the most enduring symbols of winter in Steamboat. Skijoring was an exhibition event in 1915, with competitors driving their own horses during the Saturday competition. At subsequent carnivals, skijoring contestants have been pulled by dogs, bicycles and even cars. According to Sureva Towler's *The History of Skiing at Steamboat Springs*, two men—one driving a Studebaker and one driving a Nash, pulled racing

Competitors duke it out in the "ladies' free-for-all" race at the first winter carnival, 1914.

skiers down a 500-yard course past the Cabin Hotel in 1926. But as Jean Wren pointed out in *Steamboat Springs and the Treacherous and Speedy Skee*, "a speedy quarter horse was and still is the favorite, shod for ice and ridden down Lincoln Avenue at full speed, hooves kicking up stinging pellets of snow."

Marvin Crawford, who competed in dozens of winter carnivals, remembers going down to Lincoln Avenue prior to the skijoring races "to look at the horses and try to pick out the fastest one. But of course every other kid in town was down there doing the same thing."

When the jumping competition came around on Sunday afternoon, it became the focus of the weekend. "We don't get nearly the crowds now that we had then—not even close," says Moose Barrows. (Many of the spectators would take the ski train from Denver, which stopped running in 1966.) "A guy named Walt Webber used to drive around with this big sound machine on top of his truck with speakers three feet high that he'd use to blow everybody away. He'd start off at 7 in the morning, and he had the town so pumped up they were going nuts by noon."

Barrows adds that the carnivals were a lot different when he was a kid, with more emphasis placed on beating the other guy. "There was none of this 'be fair to everybody' stuff," Barrows says. "You had to go down there and fend for yourself. You wanted a horse that was fast, and you wanted a guy who could pull you as fast as you could go."

A third day was added to the carnival in 1916, as were two traditions that remain a major part of the contemporary celebration—the parade and the crowning of the Carnival Queen. The 1916 carnival also marked the first time the national jumping distance record was set at Howelsen

Skijoring remains one of the most popular carnival events, although competitors are sometimes pulled by something other than a horse.

An event witnessed by a carnival crowd estimated to be around 3,000 people. By 1922, dogsled racing was added on Lincoln Avenue; the following year saw the addition of the "tug-of-war on skis." In 1927, the Ladies' Recreational Club started the first Diamond Hitch Parade, in which four skiers are pulled behind a horse—or, in recent years, behind a four-wheel-drive vehicle or a snowmobile—and judged on theme, costumes and skiing ability. In 1928, skijoring competitors were allowed to sit in a chair attached to skis; the next year snow sculptures first first were added to the mix.

One of the more colorful blunders in carnival history occurred during the Hazard Race of 1930, when Casey See had to take apart a barrel to free a couple pudgy young boys who had both crammed into the barrel at the same time and got stuck inside.

The Merrill Trophy was introduced during the 1932 carnival, awarded to the jumper with the longest 90-meter jump at Howelsen Hill. The award was established by Marcellus Merrill, an engineer, inventor and one of Carl Howelsen's first students. While Merrill is famous for inventing and patenting such items as the tire-balancing machine and the three-pin cross-country ski binding, he may be best known in Steamboat for inventing the rollers that allowed the Steamboat Springs marching band to "ski" during its summer performances.

The Steamboat Springs marching band made its carnival debut in 1935. Gerald McGuire, the band director, decided that since his band members "skied as well or better than they played," they might as well perform on skis. Prompted by the vision of the band on skis, the town was dubbed "Ski Town

USA by a Chicago sportswriter in 1947, who noted that the town had "1,700 residents and 1,685 skiers."

Many of Steamboat's biggest names in skiing put in their time with the band, including Olympian Marvin Crawford. "The highlight was the summer of 1950," Crawford says. "I played the trumpet, and we represented the Colorado State Lions Club at the International Lions Club convention in Chicago. We skied seven miles down Michigan Avenue in July. Fortunately, we had fairly light uniforms because it was really hot."

One of the most beloved carnival traditions started in 1936: the Lighted Man. Claudius Banks was an electrician from Vernal, Utah, who used his skills to create the Lighted Man costume—a harness filled with sockets for dozens of lights and a backpack that carried a car battery to power it all. The costume initially consisted of only lighted poles, but it evolved over the years to include such accoutrements as a lighted helmet, skis, Roman candles and various amounts of fireworks. Claudius skied in almost every carnival for 42 years, before passing on the duties in 1978 to his son, Jon, who continues his annual Lighted Man performance to the delight of carnival goers.

In 1975, Leif Howelsen, Carl Howelsen's son, was an honorary guest of the 63rd winter carnival. "Crowds on both sides of Lincoln Avenue waved and cheered," recalled Howelsen in *The Flying Norseman*, a biography of his father. "Embarrassment and joy went through me as I waved back to the people, smiling like a politician in an election campaign."

Anders Haugen was also honored that day, not only

Top: The Steamboat marching band, which made its first appearance at winter carnival in 1935.
Bottom: Two carnival princesses smile for the crowd.

because he and his brother had come from Wisconsin to compete in the third winter carnival in 1916, but also because he was then, and remains today, the first and only winner of an Olympic jumping medal for the United States. Though Haugen took third place at the Chamonix Olympics in 1924, he wasn't awarded his bronze medal until over 50 years later, when a researcher discovered the error while reviewing old Olympic files.

Today's winter carnival includes some of the same events that appeared in 1914, but also more modern competitions like geländesprung, snowboarding, the world's only muzzle-loading ski biathlon, ice hockey, dual-slalom bike races and the 25-yard Dog and Dad Dash, where children are pulled to the finish line first by the family dog and second by the family dad.

To ensure that there is enough snow for all these street events, piles of it are dumped in various vacant lots around town in the weeks leading up to the carnival. Then dump trucks are dispatched to spread the snow on Saturday so that it covers Lincoln Avenue from Fifth Street to 11th Street, where it is then groomed to carnival competition standards. &

Claudius Banks first created Lighted Man in 1936—it's a tradition that is still carried on today by his son, Jon, though the costume has evolved.

Above: Buddy Werner here racing at Kitzbühel, Austria, was a favorite of ski racing fans around the world.
Opposite page: Intense focus at one of the first pro races in the early '70s. Left to right: Moose Barrows, Billy Kidd, Jake Hoeschler, and Spider Sabich.

Magazine, the editors wrote of Buddy: "To the younger generation of American skiers, he is an example of dogged persistence, athletic skill and courage. To the older generation, particularly those who nursed the sport through its infancy, he represents the progress American skiing has made over the years."

In his final Olympic Games in 1964, Buddy watched teammates Billy Kidd and Jimmie Heuga win silver and bronze in the slalom, while he finished eighth in the same race. On April 12 of that year, Buddy was killed in an avalanche near St. Moritz, Switzerland, while filming a ski movie for Willy Bogner, Jr., himself an Olympian and son of the famed clothing manufacturer. "The thing that impressed me most about Buddy," wrote then U.S. Ski Team coach Bob Beattie in a remembrance in *SKIING* Magazine in 1964, "was...the way he was loved. In Europe every train conductor wanted his autograph. If he fell, all the fans would say, 'Poor Bud, he has such bad luck.' Of all the international racers he was the one they all pulled for to win. He never sulked when he lost, even though he hated losing more than anyone I've ever known. He never offered any excuses."

One of the biggest seeds for future competitive success in Steamboat was planted in January 1958, when Audrey Light Temple called a meeting at her house for the purpose of forming a ski club for small children. A half dozen women responded, including Donna Struble and Frances Nash, and

before the night was over, the women had formed a ski club for preschoolers called Little Toots. The group hired Crosby Perry-Smith to give once-a-week ski lessons at 50 cents per lesson per child. Later that spring, the Little Toots held what was possibly the first four-event ski meet for preschoolers—the Little Toots Regatta—on the hill behind the elementary school. Bobby Struble and Clarinda Perry-Smith took home the Skimeister trophies (for earning the highest combined point total in the four events) and Jeff Temple won the boys' jumping contest with a leap of six feet.

The first ski races on Storm Mountain were held the following spring, in 1959, when University of Wyoming hosted races on runs that are now called See Me and Voo Doo. Storm Mountain founder Jim Temple raced in one of the events against Chuck Leckenby, editor of the *Steamboat Pilot*. "I remember I beat Chuck in a slalom race up there in '58 or '59," Temple says. "Which is probably why that race never made it into the paper."

Dozens of Steamboat's most successful skiers went on to

Crosby Perry-Smith (under start banner) taught the first Little Toots class and organized the first race, shown here in June 1958.

compete at the collegiate level, with many of them ending up at either the University of Denver—under the tutelage of Willy Schaeffler—or at the University of Colorado, under Bob Beattie. The German-born Schaeffler was "tough, tough, tough," says Willis Nash. "He fought in the French resistance, and he had these scars all over him. He'd make us run back and forth across the football field, and there was no quitting time. I don't know how old he was when he was coaching us, but he could run us ragged."

Later it was Beattie who coached the likes of Moose Barrows, Jere Elliott and Billy Kidd. "Schaeffler won a lot of national championships but he would always recruit a bunch of European kids to help him do it," Kidd says of the legendary showdowns between CU and DU. "So when we eventually won it with a team of Americans, we were really proud."

In 1968, the NCAA Ski Championships were held on Howelsen Hill, and ABC's *Wide World of Sports* sent

commentator Jim McKay and a camera crew to cover the event. "That was the first major alpine competition to take place in Steamboat," says Mix Beauvais. "There weren't any real major races taking place anywhere in the West at that time...so it was a big deal for us."

In 1970, Bob Beattie's pro ski tour came to Steamboat for the first time. In the years that followed, Steamboat would become a regular stop on the professional ski racing tour, with several locals competing in front of their hometown crowd.

Lonny Vanatta, a Steamboat native who graduated all the way from Little Toots to the pro tour, never qualified for an Olympics, but he did manage to win an unprecedented 20 professional races. Vanatta was the World Professional Slalom Champion in 1980, during which time he joined Hank Kashiwa as a touring pro for the Steamboat ski area. Kashiwa, who won the overall pro title in 1975, is one of the many Steamboat residents who began his career elsewhere

Below top: Hank Kashiwa was a touring pro for Steamboat ski area and the World Champion in 1975, edging out Frenchman Henri Duvillard.
Below bottom: Sven Wiik played a major role in the growth of Nordic skiing.

Opposite page: Olympic silver medalist Travis Mayer.
Below: Steamboat native Lonny Vanatta won 20 races on the pro ski tour in the '70s and '80s.

but found success while rooted in the Yampa Valley.

Sven Wiik is another Steamboat transplant, but one who has had such a strong influence it seems he's been in the valley forever. Wiik was a gymnastics competitor in the 1948 summer Olympics in London, and moved to Colorado from his native Sweden in 1949 to become ski coach at Western State College in Gunnison (where he coached Steamboat's Pete Wither, among others). By 1956, three of Wiik's students were on the U.S. Olympic team, and by 1960 he was coaching

it. In 1969, Wiik retired from WSC, and he and his wife bought 16 acres of land next to the Steamboat ski area and opened the Scandinavian Lodge—a resort and cross-country touring center. Wiik played a major role in the growth of Nordic skiing in the valley, volunteering many hours to the Steamboat Springs Winter Sports Club and founding the Rabbit Ears Stampede, a 50-kilometer April ski marathon.

Today, the spirit of competition remains alive and well in Steamboat, with the annual Town Challenge races bringing dozens of locals to both Howelsen Hill and Mount Werner to compete for a host of prizes provided by local businesses. And modern Olympians like Ann Battelle, Nelson Carmichael, Caroline Lalive, Johnny Spillane, Shannon Dunn, Todd Lodwick, young jumper Clint Jones and 2002 Olympic silver medalist Travis Mayer continue to carry the competitive flame to the ultimate winter sporting event. ✷

This page: Modern Olympians (clockwise from top left): Ann Battelle, Nelson Carmichael, Todd Lodwick, Travis Mayer and Caroline Lalive. Opposite page: Kris "Fuzz" Feddersen, was the top-ranked World Cup aerialist in '84, '85 and '87.

171

Chapter 7

Steamboat Summer

Summer backpacking in the 235,000-acre Flat Tops Wilderness
Area—the second-largest wilderness area in Colorado.

Driving down the west side of Rabbit Ears Pass, gazing over the Yampa Valley as a late April afternoon blends spring into summer, you may find it hard to keep your eyes on the road. To the left is Catamount Lake, its edges just starting to thaw, exposing trout-filled feeding lanes. The Flat Tops Wilderness is visible to the southwest, reminding you of that backpacking trip you've got planned for July. And below you is the Yampa River, weaving its way toward town, just begging to be fished, paddled or played in.

For all the fun to be found in Steamboat in winter, there is an equal amount to be had in spring and summer. Maybe more, in fact. Steamboat is one of the finest multisport towns on earth. On a typical day in April, an ambitious person can ski the mountain in the morning, mountain bike at midday, paddle the Yampa in the afternoon and still have time to catch an evening bite on the river.

In 1990, Steamboat Ski & Resort Corp. opened its trails on the mountain for hiking and mountain biking, answering the dreams of many who'd long drooled over the

The view southwest to the Flat Tops from Rabbit Ears Pass, looking over Catamount Lake.

Summer wildflowers on Rabbit Ears Pass.

thought of loading a bike onto the gondola for the ride up (hikers can also ride the gondola daily throughout the summer). Ski patrol director Pete Wither played a major role in that decision and spent summers working as head of mountain bike operations. Pete's Wicked Trail, a burly ride down Mount Werner, is named in his honor. Not all the trails are steep, however. The mountain offers a variety of both double- and single-track routes, from casual cruisers to hairpin technical descents. The interest in mountain biking spread quickly, and today visitors can rent bikes at the base of the resort—near the rock-climbing wall and the bungee-jump trampoline—and ride over 50 miles of maintained trails. For a more mellow experience, bikers can pedal the paved Yampa Valley Core Trail, which follows the Yampa River through town.

Many mountain bikers rejoiced again in the fall of 1997, when the Mountain View trail was completed from Long Lake to the top of Mount Werner. The trail made it possible for

bikers to ride ridgetops from Rabbit Ears Pass to the top of the ski area, weaving through fields of wildflowers and past spectacular vistas, covering more than 20 miles before ending with a 3,000-foot descent down Mount Werner. The Town Challenge Mountain Bike Series continues to be a favorite among local racers. The televised Mercury Tour mountain bike race came to town from 1997 to 2000, even drawing superstar Lance Armstrong, though he didn't do very well. For runners, there's the annual Steamboat marathon and half marathon, which begins north of town at Hahns Peak and has been called one of the most scenic races in the country.

A "competition" from the '70s that's still talked about in Steamboat was the Tugboat River Race. Started in 1975 with about 300 entrants, it grew to "5,000 in the river, 5,000 watching it and three helicopters flying over the water," says Larry Lamb, whose Tugboat Saloon sponsored the event. "We literally had people coming from around the world to participate," Lamb says. "They'd show up with

Opposite page: Dozens of Steamboat mountain bike trails lead riders through stands of aspen.
Below: Negotiating the technical descent of the Fish Creek Falls trail.

A poster announcing the first official road race in Steamboat, organized in 1975 by Mountain Bike Hall of Famer Kent Eriksen.

Above: The annual Tugboat River Race drew hundreds of people to town in the mid 1970s, with some revelers coming from across the country. Opposite page: Horse packing into the high country is a popular activity in Northwest Colorado.

their craft, or they'd construct it on-site, but they'd get something in the water. We had people put Volkswagens on top of inner tubes and some people just swim it."

Sometimes the difficulty in predicting Yampa River levels made for logistical difficulties on the water. "We never picked a date for the race until a week or two before it happened, because it all depended on the height of the river—too high and you couldn't get under the bridges, too low and you couldn't get down," says Lamb. "One year these guys showed up with an 18-person paddle craft—the river was pretty high and they hit the first bridge and 17 people went in the water. The only person left on the boat going across the finish line was Billy Kidd." After a nearly decade-long run, concerns about safety and the river ecosystem caused organizers to end the Tugboat River Race in 1983.

While rafting, mountain biking, fishing, hiking, golf and a multitude of other summer activities still keep even the most active resident or visitor entertained, part of what makes Steamboat such a great ski town in the summertime is what it doesn't have—a national park. Though there are thousands of acres of wilderness and national forest nearby, without a national park, Steamboat just doesn't draw the large crowds of summer visitors that flock to a Jackson, Wyoming, or a Whitefish, Montana.

South of Steamboat lies the 235,000-acre Flat Tops Wilderness, the second-largest wilderness area in Colorado,

where hikers and backpackers can choose from 40 trailheads, 80 lakes and the more than 200 miles of trails that wind through both the Routt and White River national forests—including the Devils Causeway, a slim ridge trail that narrows to four feet in places.

Though it wasn't the first wilderness area in the nation, Flat Tops was actually the hatching ground for the concept of roadless wilderness areas. A U.S. Forest Service employee named Arthur Carhart was dispatched to the Flat Tops from Denver in 1919, charged with mapping 100 homesites around Trappers Lake. A trained architect, Carhart returned to Denver with the recommendation that the area be preserved instead of built on.

The 27-year-old Carhart met with Aldo Leopold, who was then an assistant district forester in Albuquerque, New Mexico. Leopold asked Carhart to summarize his thoughts in writing, and, in 1920, Carhart wrote: "There are a number

Though outfits seemed to matter as much as outcome, the Tugboat River Race did manage to raise thousands of dollars for local charities over the years.

of places with scenic values of such great worth that they are rightfully the property of all people. They should be preserved for all time for the people of the nation and the world. Trappers Lake is unquestionably a candidate for that classification." Leopold is generally credited with helping New Mexico's Gila Wilderness Area become the nation's first wilderness preserve in 1924. Carhart's writings became frequent resources and influential documents in the eventual creation of the Wilderness Act of 1964.

Northeast of town is Steamboat's other neighborhood wilderness area, the Zirkels. Mount Zirkel Wilderness is a 159,935-acre alpine playground featuring countless wild-flowers, dozens of lakes and over 150 miles of hiking trails straddling the Continental Divide. The area experienced an intense natural phenomenon in 1997 when winds in excess of 120 miles per hour came barreling down from the Divide, flattening more than four million trees in a path 30 miles long and nearly five miles wide. Because the incident—later termed the "Routt Divide Blowdown"—occurred in late

Mount Zirkel Wilderness is a 159,935-acre alpine playground featuring countless wildflowers, dozens of lakes and over 150 miles of hiking trails straddling the Continental Divide.

Opposite page: The majestic Flat Tops, birthplace of the American wilderness ideal.
Below: Horse packing north of Steamboat in the 159,935-acre Mount Zirkel Wilderness Area is a popular way to cover a lot of ground.

The Yampa River

By Eugene Buchanan

Perhaps nothing defines the town of Steamboat as well as the river that runs through it, carrying Mount Werner's snowmelt down through town and across the Dinosaur National Monument until it merges with the Green and, eventually, Colorado rivers. The Yampa River (early trappers called it the Bear River) has been the lifeblood of the valley ever since early Ute Indians named it after the area's nourishing yampa roots. Since then, it has continued serving that role, nourishing everything from local ranch land and snow-making capabilities for the ski area to the recreational needs of fly-fishers, kayakers and even inner-tubers.

Ecologically, the river is as diverse as the locals living along its banks. It's the country's only river with breeding habitat for the world's largest minnow, the Colorado River pike (formerly known as the squawfish), and is only one of three in the entire Colorado River Basin with a rare natural mix of narrowleaf cottonwood, red osier dogwood and box elder. When combined with the White River drainage downstream, it has the highest volume of discharge (1,623,000 acre-feet) for its surface area in the world.

The river's impact on the community is just as huge as the region's snowfall. Fly-fishers regularly traipse its waters from below Stagecoach Reservoir to its confluence with the Elk in search of brown, rainbow and brook trout, with more than five outfitters offering guided excursions.

"It's definitely an unsung secret of Colorado," says fly-fishing guide Hans Berend. "There are a bunch of different sections you can fish, either as a quick fix during lunch break or as a full-on float trip."

As it courses through town, wending past soccer fields, softball diamonds and parks, the river passes beneath the decks of several local establishments that wisely use its ambience for dinner and drinks. The aptly named Yacht Club overlooks its banks, as does the Cottonwood Grill. Each spring, the Yampa buries three hot springs under snowmelt, which resurface later to once again gurgle from the banks and become part of a popular hot springs tour for tourists.

To help celebrate the river's place in the hearts of townsfolk, the city, through a nonprofit organization called Friends of the Yampa, stages an annual river festival every June in its honor. Best likened as a version of the town's annual winter carnival, the celebration includes a variety of canoe and kayak races, fly-casting clinics, Dutch-oven cook-offs and other events designed to raise awareness for the watershed. This past summer's event celebrated the building of a new play hole for local kayakers, which was so successful that sandal giant Teva used it as a stop on its national freestyle tour. Garnering just as much attention, of course, was the annual Crazy

Top: Floating in a driftboat is a popular way to access quality trout fishing water.
Bottom: Prolific bug hatches draw many a fly-fisher to the Yampa River.

Riverdog Contest, a zany event timing local dogs' ability to retrieve sticks from the river.

Just like playing with gravity on the ski slopes above it, running the river for recreation is also steeped in tradition. *Paddler* Magazine moved its offices a block away from the Yampa in 1992, and named Steamboat as one of the top paddling towns in the country in a 1994 feature story. Of course, the town's river-running roots extend far deeper. Just downstream in 1909, Nathaniel Galloway, who developed the upstream-ferry technique for running whitewater, first ran the sandstone corridor of Yampa Canyon. In the 1960s, the lower Yampa became the battleground for one of the water conservationists' biggest victories, with the Sierra Club's David Brower leading the fight to save Yampa and Gates of Lodore canyons from two dams—at Echo Park and at Split Mountain—that would have buried them and Dinosaur National Park forever.

The river has also laid claim to more modern-day, river-running heroes, giving reason for some to start calling Ski Town USA "Paddle Town USA." While Steamboat is home to dozens of Olympians, one you don't often hear about is the late slalom kayaker Rich Weiss, who used to chip ice from the river's banks in winter to train for what would eventually become spots on the 1992 and '96 Summer Olympic teams (he finished sixth in the latter). Weiss also became the first American to medal in men's kayak at a World Championships event, taking the silver in 1993 in Italy. Weiss was killed in a kayaking accident in the Northwest in 1997, and a town park next to the river was officially renamed in his honor at a ceremony in 2000, complete with the unveiling of a statue of him kayaking.

Numerous outfitters have also called the Yampa Valley home, including Colorado Adventures (now the popular Sheri Griffith Adventures in Moab, Utah) and Wild West River Riders. "Steamboat's a haven for them because of its access to the desert canyons," says longtime local Barry Smith, an 11-year Grand Canyon river guide who moved here in 1974 and now runs one of the town's two kayak schools. "It really is a special resource." &

Eugene Buchanan is the editor-in-chief of Paddler *magazine.*

The Yampa provides one of the longest stretches of free-flowing river in the country, running unencumbered for more than 200 miles from just southeast of Steamboat to its confluence with the Green, near the Utah state line.

October instead of the more busy summer months of July or August, few people were in the area at the time. Some salvage logging took place in the non-wilderness sections of the blowdown, but visitors to the region can still plainly see the effects of this bizarre natural act.

Closer to town, there are several great day hikes to choose from, including Spring Creek or the popular Fish Creek Falls, where the creek tumbles 283 feet on its way to the Yampa. For flower lovers, the Yampa River Botanic Park is a series of 30 distinct gardens open dawn to dusk from May 1 through October 31. The property for the park was donated to the town in 1991, and the park opened in 1997, providing an opportunity for an afternoon stroll among several sculptures and dozens of native Colorado species found along the Yampa, from the alpine zones of the Flat Tops to the semidesert regions of southeastern Utah.

Visitors to the botanic park may also catch classical music as part of the resort's Young Artists in Residence program. The Music on the Green concert series is just one of the many offerings of Strings in the Mountains, a program that was launched in 1988 to bring world-class contemporary and classical music to Steamboat. The summerlong performances, which take place on the mountain near the Slopeside Bar and Grill, include more than 150 different artists throughout the season. Since that first summer, attendance has grown from 1,400 people to more than 30,000.

Not that classical is the only kind of music floating through the valley on a summer night. Steamboat offers one of the best concert lineups in the Rockies, with popular artists playing free shows that alternate between the Steamboat ski resort and Howelsen Hill from late June through September. There's also a mix of other concerts and music festivals that come to town throughout the summer, ranging over the years from the hippie grooves of String Cheese Incident to the soulful sounds of James Brown (after whom a bridge over the Yampa is named) to the country tunes of Clint Black.

Surrounded as it is by authentic Western heritage, no summer visit to Steamboat would be complete without taking

Opposite page: Fish Creek Falls, just north of town, plunges nearly 300 feet on its way to the Yampa.
Below: Bright red Indian Paintbrush, one of the many native wildflowers of the Yampa Valley.

in a rodeo. For 16 years, the valley has been hosting the Pro Rodeo series at Romick Arena at Howelsen Hill, with professional cowboys and cowgirls competing every weekend from the end of June through August in a variety of events such as steer wrestling, bull riding, team roping and bareback and saddle bronc riding.

"The cowboys existed in Steamboat long before the marketing concept," says Lance Romick, eldest of the three rodeo-loving Romick brothers—all of whom were also successful ski racers (youngest brother Jace made the U.S. Ski Team when he was 17 and was the number-one ranked downhiller in the country in 1982). "It was a pretty natural transition for us boys when we were growing up—after you hung your skis up in the spring, you'd just go get on your horse."

Rodeos have been taking place in the Yampa Valley since the late 1800s, but trail rides and dude ranches have also added to both the image and the reality of Steamboat's Western identity. "Most small towns have a legacy of some type," says Romick. "In the Northeast it might be fishing, in

> "The cowboys existed in Steamboat long before the marketing concept. It was a pretty natural transition for us boys when we were growing up— after you hung your skis up in the spring, you'd just go get on your horse."

Opposite page: A bronc rider hangs on for life at the Romick Arena. The Pro Rodeo series takes place every weekend throughout the summer. Below: A proper dismount is obviously crucial when coming down off a bucking bull. Rodeo clowns help lure the bull away from the rider.

the Northwest logging. Here it's ranching."

Cowboy Pat Mantle was just one individual who did much to enhance that legacy, moving to town in 1971 and opening the Sombrero Stables, offering trail rides to hundreds of tourists over the course of 30 years. "Pat owned more horses than anyone in the United States," Romick says. "And he supplied them for both sport and leisure, rodeo or trail ride."

Anyone who enjoys the wide streets of Steamboat has the tradition of cattle drives to thank for it. Though the drives now take place more for the benefit of tourists than for practical ranching reasons, seeing a couple hundred head of "beef-on-the-hoof"—as author John Rolfe Burroughs described them—is still something to behold. The 2003 summer will mark the 100th anniversary of the annual Cowboy Roundup and Fourth of July Celebration, including fireworks and a cattle drive through downtown.

If bucking broncs or roping competitions aren't your thing, there are other types of rodeos available. In mid June,

kayakers compete in the annual Fat Eddy's whitewater rodeo, held on the Yampa River just downstream from the Bud Werner Memorial Library. And Steamboat's annual Hot Air Balloon Rodeo has been taking place every July since 1981, offering—for those who can get up early—spectacular views of approximately 50 balloons taking to the sky at dawn. The Balloon Rodeo usually coincides with Art in the Park, a weekend event offering visitors dozens of creative offerings in West Lincoln Park.

Balloons sometimes share the sky with hang gliders, which have been circling the Yampa Valley since the early '70s. The sport is promoted and regulated by the Storm Peak Hang Gliding Association, which gets needed backing from a national governing body, the U.S. Hang Gliders Association in Colorado Springs. "They provide us with insurance, which allows us to fly, and a rating program, so we can make sure young pilots are qualified," says Storm Peak Hang Gliding Association president, Tom Wood.

Below top: Hang gliding has been a precarious but popular activity on Mount Werner since the early 1970s.
Below bottom: Many waves and holes on the Yampa are filled with kayakers.

Opposite page: The annual Hot Air Balloon Rodeo has taken place in Steamboat for more than 20 years.
Below: Cowboy Pat Mantle opened the Sombrero Stables in 1971.

The importance of a rating and evaluation system was never more clear than when a local hang glider named Anthony Mathews died after falling out of a homemade glider in the mid 1970s. The accident caused authorities to ban hang gliding in the valley until an agreement between the Forest Service, the ski resort and the Storm Peak Hang Gliding Association allowed the sport to continue. "We have a special use permit from the Forest Service," Wood says. "That allowed us to get the mountain opened up again at Thunderhead, which is our main launch site, but it's an expert-rated launch because of the gondola and because of all the storms that roll in. It can be an ugly place for beginners."

In spring of 1971, LTV opened the Robert Trent Jones Jr.–designed Steamboat Golf Club (now called the Sheraton Steamboat Golf Club) near the mountain. It is now one of three public courses in the valley, but the only one with Fish Creek winding past seven of the holes. East of town lies the Haymaker Golf Course and to the west lies the oldest of the three, the *original* Steamboat Golf Club, built in 1964. The Catamount Ranch and Club offers the only private course in town. There's also a new kind of golf available—disc golf at the Steamboat ski area—free to anyone with a Frisbee.

Regardless of which activity you choose, nothing satisfies like a dip in the Strawberry Park Hot Springs after a summer day of self-induced labor. Located seven miles north of town on 40 acres of land bordering national forest, these outdoor springs have almost become synonymous with relaxation in

Opposite page: Catamount Golf Course, showcasing the lush green of an early spring. Catamount is one of four golf courses in the area. Below: The soothing water of Strawberry Hot Springs.

A bright autumn day in Routt County—the perfect time for a horseback ride in the mountains.

Steamboat. The springs emerge from the earth at almost 150 degrees Fahrenheit but are cooled after mixing with creek water. Separate pools are divided by beautiful masonry work and small waterfalls, each with varying temperatures, the warmest averaging a perfect muscle-soaking 104 degrees. ✳

Regardless of which activity you choose, nothing satisfies like a dip in the Strawberry Park Hot Springs after a summer day of self-induced labor.

The Olympians

Y ou've heard it dozens of times before: No town has produced more Winter Olympians than Steamboat Springs, Colorado. From ski jumpers to snowboarders, alpine racers to aerialists, Ski Town USA knows how to send athletes to the ultimate winter sporting event. There are 47 total, as of fall 2002, and this doesn't include four nonresidents —Nick Cleaver and Maria Despas (Australia), Jorge Torruella (Puerto Rico) and Linas Vaitkus (Lithuania), who trained with the Steamboat Springs Winter Sports Club but skied for their home countries in the Olympics. Nor does it include the likes of Billy Kidd, Sven Wiik, Hank Kashiwa or Chris Puckett— Olympic athletes who were living elsewhere when they went to the Games but who now call Steamboat home. From John Steele, who became Steamboat's first Olympian in 1932, to 2002 Olympic silver medalist Travis Mayer (below), here are the athletes who helped put Steamboat on the map.

Some of the many Olympians who have called Steamboat home gathered together for a little reunion prior to the 2002 Winter Games in Salt Lake City, Utah.

Alan Alborn

Born: 1980

Olympic Years: 1998, 2002

Team: Ski Jumping

Alan "Airborne" Alborn is an Alaska native who started training with the Steamboat Springs Winter Sports Club shortly after the family moved to Colorado in 1994. He is tied in second place with Ted Farwell for the most Olympic finishes by a Steamboat athlete—six—just behind Todd Lodwick, who has seven. (The great alpine racer Buddy Werner competed in six Olympic events, but he finished only four of them.) Like his father, Alborn is a pilot, flying his own Cessna when he's not flying on skis. In 2001, while training in Oberstdorf, Germany, he became the first American to jump farther than 200 meters (656 feet), and achieved his personal ski-flying best in March of 2002 when he flew 221.5 meters (726.7 feet). Alborn was the top American jumper at the Salt Lake Olympics, finishing 11th in the individual K90 event. He wrapped up his 2002 season by winning both the K90 and K120 national titles at the U.S. Ski Jumping Championships at Howelsen Hill.

Jim "Moose" Barrows

Born: 1944

Olympic Year: 1968

Team: Alpine

Moose Barrows might be best known as the original "Agony of Defeat" guy for ABC's *Wide World of Sports*. Barrows' fall in the downhill at the 1968 Olympics in Grenoble, France, opened the show until 1973, when it was replaced by an even more spectacular crash—that of Czechoslovakian ski jumper Finko Bogatosh. Barrows had the fortune (or misfortune) of competing against the great Jean-Claude Killy, an overwhelming presence at the '68 Games. Barrows is almost a Steamboat native, arriving as a six-year-old in 1951, when his father opened a gas station on Highway 40. He is a graduate of the University of Colorado, where he won the Schoenberger Award for all-around excellence in academics and athletics, after which he became the recreation director at Steamboat ski resort from 1971 to 1976. Moose turned pro in 1970, finishing 10th in earnings with $4,390. He still lives in Steamboat.

Ann Battelle

Born: 1968

Olympic Years: 1992, 1994, 1998, 2002

Team: Freestyle

Battelle is a four-time Olympian and two-time World Cup mogul champion, despite the fact that she didn't even start mogul skiing until after she graduated from Vermont's Middlebury College, where she also played soccer. She moved to Steamboat shortly after college to attend Park Smalley's Great Western Freestyle Center (she later coached at his camp at Mount Hood, Oregon). She won the 1999 World Mogul Championships and has more than 20 top-three World Cup finishes. Battelle won both gold and silver medals at the 2000 Goodwill Games.

Scott Berry

Born: 1948

Olympic Year: 1972

Team: Ski Jumping

Ski jumper Scott Berry was the only Steamboat representative at the '72 Games in Sapporo, Japan—less than six months after the infamous "Munich Massacre" at the Summer Games in Munich, Germany, where 11 Israelis were killed by Arab terrorists. It had been 24 years since Steamboat had sent only one person—Gordy Wren—to the Olympics. Berry finished in 47th place on the large hill and 52nd on the small hill, which were then 90-meter and 70-meter, respectively. He won the Harris Memorial Trophy in 1971 and took third in the U.S. National Jumping Championships in 1972.

Van Card

Born: 1939

Olympic Year: 1964

Team: Ski Jumping

Card is one of the many talented jumpers to train under both Al Wegeman and Gordy Wren, winning the U.S. Junior National Slalom Championships in 1957 before going on to ski for Bob Beattie's NCAA Championships team at the University of Colorado. After college and a trip to the Innsbruck Olympics in 1964, Card returned to Steamboat and became the head jump coach for the Steamboat Springs Winter Sports Club from 1964 to 1966. Card also coached both skiing and soccer at Yampa Valley College, and became the athletic director at Colorado Alpine College (later named Colorado Mountain College), when the school hosted the NCAA Championships.

Nelson Carmichael

Born: 1965

Olympic Years: 1988, 1992

Team: Freestyle

A top competitor in both aerials and moguls, Carmichael became the first Steamboat resident to win an Olympic medal—a bronze in moguls at the 1992 Games in Albertville, France. Carmichael moved to Steamboat from Ohio in 1977, and eight years later won the U.S. National Mogul Championship. He won it again in 1987 and was one of the most consistent mogul skiers in the country throughout the 1980s. When Carmichael was a senior in high school, he became the first skier to win both the bumps and the aerial competition at the Tequila Cup, when he took both crowns in 1983. He now spends winters working for the Steamboat ski resort and summers windsurfing in Hood River, Oregon.

Gary Crawford

Born: 1957

Olympic Years: 1980, 1988

Team: Nordic Combined

Though no relation to the famed Crawfords who settled the town in the 19th century, Steamboat native Gary Crawford nevertheless comes from a family with deep Yampa Valley roots. His grandfather moved to Steamboat to practice medicine in 1936, and his father, Marvin, is not only a member of the Colorado Ski Hall of Fame, but also was one of the founding partners of the original Storm Mountain ski area. Crawford skied at Western State College and was on the U.S. Nordic Combined Team for almost 20 years before becoming head jump coach for the Steamboat Springs Winter Sports Club. Crawford still lives in Steamboat, where he spends summers as head pro at the Sheraton Steamboat Golf Club.

Marvin Crawford

Born: 1932

Olympic Years: 1952, 1956

Teams: Ski Jumping, Nordic, Nordic Combined

Marvin Crawford had done plenty of skiing by the time he became the first manager of the Storm Mountain ski area in 1964. Fifteen years earlier, he'd set the National Class C distance record for skiers under 18 when he jumped 190 feet at Howelsen Hill. He won 14 national championships competing in four disciplines: jumping, cross-country, slalom and downhill—and he never lost in four-way competition. Crawford was also the jump instructor at Winter Park from 1957 to 1963 and was inducted into the Colorado Ski Hall of Fame in 1981. He began his college career on a scholarship at the University of Washington, but he transferred to the University of Denver after the first quarter. "I was walking to class and it was raining—again," Crawford says. "So I called Willy Schaeffler at the University of Denver to see if he still wanted me to come there and ski. He said yes, so the next quarter I transferred."

Jeff Davis

Born: 1958

Olympic Year: 1980

Team: Ski Jumping

Another veteran of Western State College in Gunnison, Colorado, Davis, a Steamboat native, was "one of the best jumpers ever to emerge from the Rocky Mountain Division," according to the 1980 U.S. Ski Team media guide. On March 8, 1981, Davis "added a shot of adrenaline to the entire U.S. Ski Jumping program" when he took first place in Lahti, Finland, setting a new hill record. He finished 17th in the 70-meter jump at the Lake Placid Olympics.

Brendan Doran

Born: 1979

Olympic Years: 1998, 2002

Team: Ski Jumping

Doran grew up playing soccer in Southern California and was once a member of the New York State All-Star soccer team. But since moving to Steamboat with his family when he was nine, he has focused on ski jumping and the occasional turkey hunt with his dad. His first big victory came in 1995 when he won the Continental Cup in Westby, Wisconsin, before going on to compete in the 1995 World Championships. Doran was the U.S. 90-meter champion in 2000.

Shannon Dunn

Born: 1972

Olympic Year: 1998

Team: Snowboarding

By earning a bronze in halfpipe at the 1998 Nagano Games, Dunn became the first American woman ever to win an Olympic snowboarding medal. She moved to Steamboat from Chicago with her family when she was nine and broke onto the snowboard scene by winning the U.S. Open halfpipe competition at Stratton Mountain, Vermont, in 1993 and again in 1994. In addition to being a U.S. Open champ, Dunn has taken first place in halfpipe at both the X Games (2001) and the Gravity Games (2000). Her father, Jerry—a former minor league hockey player—has been an insurance agent in Steamboat for more than 20 years. Shannon married fellow snow-boarder Dave Downing in 1999, and they now spend winters in Lake Tahoe and summers in San Diego, where she participates in her other love—surfing.

Jere Elliott

Born: 1946

Olympic Year: 1968

Team: Alpine

Elliott is one of the many skiers who coach Rudi Schnackenberg convinced to add alpine to an already established set of Nordic skiing skills. The younger of the two Elliott brothers, Jere was a multisport athlete whose skills also included pole vaulting for the track squad and quarterbacking for the football team. He raced for two years for the University of Wyoming Cowboys before moving on to the University of Colorado and ultimately the U.S. Ski Team, where he competed for five years, from 1965 to 1969. Elliott joined Billy Kidd, Moose Barrows and Loris Werner on the same '68 Olympic team—but Jean-Claude Killy won everything anyway.

Jon Elliott

Born: 1941

Olympic Year: 1960

Team: Ski Jumping

Another emigrant from the flatlands of the Midwest, Elliott was a consummate promoter of cross-country skiing, working as a cross-country ski coach at Jackson Hole, Wyoming, from 1965 to 1969 and later as the director of the United States Ski Association. Like his brother, he attended the University of Wyoming in Laramie—only Jon stayed through graduation. He went on to design cross-country ski trails for various towns in Montana, California and Alaska.

Kristoffer Erichsen

Born: 1978

Olympic Years: 1998, 2002

Team: Nordic Combined

As the name would suggest, Erichsen has deep Norwegian roots. He was born in Rapid City, South Dakota, but grew up in Norway and was released by the Norwegian Ski Federation in 1995 to ski for the U.S., after which he moved to Steamboat. Though he made the Olympic team, he didn't compete in either Nagano or Salt Lake. But he did earn a World Cup B victory in Calgary in 2001 and made three other World Cup B podiums.

Ted Farwell

Born: 1934

Olympic Years: 1952, 1956, 1960

Teams: Nordic, Nordic Combined

It is sometimes easy to forget Ted Farwell in the history of great Steamboat skiers, simply because he competed in the same Olympics as bigger names like Buddy and Skeeter Werner, Marvin Crawford and Katy Rodolph-Wyatt. But he was one of the most consistent competitors in the country throughout the 1950s, with three top-12 Olympic finishes in Nordic and Nordic Combined.

Kris "Fuzz" Feddersen

Born: 1963

Olympic Years: 1988, 1992, 1994

Team: Freestyle

Feddersen, a former shortstop in his hometown of Cincinnati, was a member of the first summer camp of the Great Western Freestyle Center, in which he enrolled at age 12. He won the U.S. National Ballet Championships at Squaw Valley in 1982, but started focusing on aerials to compete on the World Cup. He took the national aerial crown in 1983, at Waterville Valley, New Hampshire. A four-time World Championships winner, Feddersen moved to Steamboat with his family when he was 10 and started doing aerials as a fifth grader when he and his friends built jumps during recess. He was the top-ranked U.S. World Cup aerialist in '84, '85 and '87. Feddersen retired midway through the 1996 season, after a decade of being a consistent top-five aerialist and a week after collecting his third World Cup victory. He has helped coach members of the U.S. Freestyle Team ever since.

Matt Grosjean

Born: 1970

Olympic Years: 1992, 1994, 1998

Team: Alpine

Grosjean was one of the many kids who moved to Steamboat as a toddler and started skiing shortly thereafter. He says he learned how to handle changing snow conditions by "shadowing older brother Marty all over Mount Werner." Though Grosjean never earned an Olympic podium, he did take 15th in Nagano, making him the top U.S. slalom finisher. (And he took third on his first combined run.) Grosjean also took first in slalom three times at the U.S. National Championships, in Winter Park ('92 and '93) and Park City ('95). He also was a two-time winner of the in-line skate slalom competition for ABC's *Wide World of Sports*.

Ryan Heckman

Born: 1974

Olympic Years: 1992, 1994

Team: Nordic Combined

Heckman started out strong and stayed that way, winning the first international competition he entered, in Calgary, Alberta, at age 15. The following season, he won the large-hill title at the 1991 U.S. Ski Jumping Championships, and the year after that he was in Albertville, France, helping the Olympic team to an eighth-place finish in Nordic Combined. One of the many skiers to graduate from Steamboat's Lowell Whiteman School (a prep school with a ski and snowboard racing program), Heckman finished 29th in the individual Nordic Combined event at the '94 Games in Lillehammer, Norway. He spent six years on the team and competed in six major championships—two Olympics and four World Championships.

Corky Heid

Born: 1935

Olympic Year: 1956

Team: Ski Jumping

Though named as an alternate to the jumping team for the Cortina Games, the older Heid brother never made it to Italy. Nevertheless, he enjoyed a successful jumping career, including taking fifth place at the U.S. National Jumping Championships in Steamboat in 1953. Heid had a huge impact on the early days of the Steamboat ski area, taking over as head of the ski patrol in 1970 and remaining at that post for 12 years. He started his ski management career at Breckenridge, where he began as a lift op and worked his way up to mountain manager.

Ray Heid

Born: 1937

Olympic Year: 1960

Team: Ski Jumping

Like his older brother, Ray Heid made an Olympic team but never got to compete—though he did forerun the course at Squaw Valley. After the Olympics, Heid became an assistant ski coach at his alma mater, the University of Wyoming. He was head coach there from 1962 to 1964. Heid spent 20 years in the ski retail business, running seven different shops—four in Breckenridge and three at Sierra Blanca (now Ski Apache) in Ruidoso, New Mexico.

Dave Jarrett

Born: 1970

Olympic Years: 1994, 1998

Team: Nordic Combined

Jarrett is the oldest of four boys and, like his 1994 Nordic Combined teammate Ryan Heckman, is a graduate of Steamboat's Lowell Whiteman School. He was the top American at the 1993 World Championships in Falun, Sweden, and he was one of the "fourth-place foursome" from the 1995 World Championships. Cross-country was always Jarrett's strong suit, and he was the fastest cross-country skier on the U.S. Team—in part because he'd been a cross-country skier his whole life and didn't start jumping until he was 13.

Clint Jones

Born: 1984

Olympic Year: 2002

Team: Ski Jumping

Jones apparently didn't see any reason to wait before he started setting records. The Steamboat Springs native became the youngest U.S. champion in any ski discipline when he won the K120 at the U.S. National Championships in March 2000, at the ripe old age of 15. At the Salt Lake Olympics, young Jones didn't qualify for the K90, but he finished 42nd in the individual K120. However, returning to Park City in September 2002, Jones beat Olympic champion Simon Ammann of Switzerland to win the 120-meter event at the Summer Grand Prix Series. It is unlikely that Jones has seen his last Olympic Games.

Caroline Lalive

Born: 1979

Olympic Years: 1998, 2002

Team: Alpine

The multiskilled Lalive has been the U.S. Ski Team's biggest threat in the alpine combined ever since she finished seventh in the event at the Nagano Olympics in 1998. She won two bronze World Cup combined medals in 2001 and repeatedly scored points in all five World Cup alpine events (slalom, GS, super G, downhill, and combined). Yet the aggressive style for which Lalive is known has also made for many a DNF (did not finish), as well as a laundry list of injuries, which have plagued her throughout her career.

Andy LeRoy

Born: 1975

Olympic Year: 1998

Team: Alpine

Though born in Steamboat, LeRoy later moved down the road to Silverthorne when his mom became general manager of the Hampton Inn there. He was the 1991 Junior Olympics GS champ and, six years later—after missing the second half of the '94–'95 season because of knee surgery—won both slalom and dual-slalom events in 1997. This helped set him up for his slalom run at the Nagano Games, though he did not finish.

Todd Lodwick

Born: 1976

Olympic Years: 1994, 1998, 2002

Team: Nordic Combined

Few Steamboat skiers have had the success Lodwick has had, which includes three Olympic appearances, more than a dozen World Cup podiums and four World Cup wins. His Nordic Combined World Cup victory in Steamboat in 1995—the first of two in front of his hometown fans—was the first for an American in 11 years. Though he didn't medal at the Salt Lake Olympics in 2002, Lodwick had three top-10 finishes, helping lead the team to fourth in the Nordic Combined, barely missing the podium.

Travis Mayer

Born: 1982

Olympic Year: 2002

Team: Freestyle

It was a happy February afternoon in Steamboat when Travis Mayer earned a silver medal at Utah's Deer Valley resort during the 2002 Olympic mogul competition. The feat was made even more memorable because Mayer had the final run of the day and bumped 1998 Olympic gold medalist Jonny Moseley from third place to fourth, despite crowd favorite Moseley successfully completing his celebrated "dinner roll" move. Mayer was the Cinderella story of the year, having just been moved up from the C team in late January after two top-three finishes. In fact, only weeks earlier, Mayer had earned his spot on the Olympic team by winning the moguls wildcard berth on New Year's Eve, at the Team Gold Cup event, also held at Deer Valley.

Chris McNeil

Born: 1954

Olympic Years: 1976, 1980

Team: Ski Jumping

McNeil received several scholarship offers in both skiing and football after graduating from Steamboat Springs High School in 1972, but instead chose to go to Europe and train with the Swiss National Jumping Team. The decision paid off, and McNeil spent eight years on the U.S. Ski Team, from 1972 to 1980, after winning the Junior Nationals Jumping Championships at Middlebury, Vermont. Though an illness kept him from competing at Innsbruck in 1976, McNeil came back four years later to take 23rd in the 70-meter jump competition at the Lake Placid Olympics. He also spent several years as the Canadian National Special Jumping Team coach.

Rick Mewborn

Born: 1965

Olympic Year: 1988

Team: Ski Jumping

The 1988 Olympics in Calgary was a showcase of diversity for the Steamboat Springs Winter Sports Club, with athletes represented on the U.S. Nordic Combined, Alpine, Jumping, and both men's and women's Freestyle teams. Mewborn was the lone representative on the Jumping Team. He'd had a great season in '85–'86, then a disappointing one in '86–'87, then came back strong in 1988 to qualify for the 70-meter event at Calgary. He spent his off-seasons working in the coal mines south of Steamboat, and once hit a cow on his motorcycle on the way home from work.

Jack Miller

Born: 1965

Olympic Year: 1988

Team: Alpine

Miller won the Junior Olympic Slalom Championships at Alpine Meadows, California, when he was 14 and won the Australian National Giant Slalom Championships in 1985, when he was 20. He was the youngest member of the U.S. Ski Team from 1984 to 1986. He was also part of the first group of students at Steamboat's Great Western Freestyle Center. (Not to mention clearing 305 feet at the 1986 gelände competition on Howelsen Hill.) Though a tailbone injury kept him out of the 1987 World Championships in Switzerland, he made it back the following year to compete in slalom and GS at the Calgary Games.

Crosby Perry-Smith

Born: 1923

Olympic Year: 1952

Team: Ski Jumping

Perry-Smith moved to Steamboat after fighting with the 10th Mountain Division in Italy during World War II. Though he didn't place at the Oslo Games in 1952, Perry-Smith returned to Steamboat and became one of the biggest coaching influences at Howelsen Hill, where he was the manager from 1957 to 1958. He coached Loris Werner, among other Olympians, and he was also the first ski instructor for the Little Toots youth ski program. In 1970 he became a jumping instructor at Winter Park, which later named their school the Crosby Perry-Smith Jumping Program

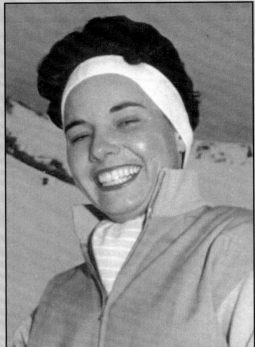

Maria Quintana

Born: 1966

Olympic Year: 1988

Team: Freestyle

Quintana began competing on the World Cup after graduating from Steamboat's Lowell Whiteman School in 1983. She was the first female skier to successfully perform a triple back flip and later won the first FIS-sanctioned World Championship gold medal for aerials, in Tignes, France, in 1986. Like many Steamboat skiers in the 1980s, Quintana was introduced to freestyle by Park Smalley at the Great Western Freestyle Center. She won her first World Cup meet at Courchevel, France, in 1984 and won another at Lake Placid in '85. Quintana retired in 1991.

Katy Rodolph-Wyatt

Born: 1930

Olympic Years: 1952, 1956

Team: Alpine

One of the most prominent female skiers in the world in the early 1950s, Rodolph-Wyatt was a nine-time winner at the U.S. National Championships, including both downhill and slalom in 1949. She was one of the many Steamboat racers taught by legendary Howelsen Hill manager Al Wegeman, whose oldest son, Paul, she married in 1951. (The marriage ended the following year.) Rodolph-Wyatt finished fifth in giant slalom at the Oslo Games and was inducted into the National Ski Hall of Fame in 1966 and the Colorado Ski Hall of Fame in 1985.

Ansten Samuelstuen

Born: 1929

Olympic Years: 1960, 1964

Team: Ski Jumping

Samuelstuen was the top U.S. finisher at the Squaw Valley Olympics in 1960—where he ended up in seventh place—nine years after breaking the U.S. jumping distance record on Howelsen Hill. (His record leap of 316 feet wasn't broken for 12 years.) A native of Norway, Samuelstuen had moved to the U.S. in 1954 at the age of 25, in part because he'd met Gordy Wren while Wren was competing in Europe. He was briefly a teammate of Marvin Crawford on Willy Schaeffler's University of Denver ski team in 1954, during Crawford's senior year. Samuelstuen went on to compete in 11 National Jumping Championships. He was a four-time Class A jumping champ at Howelsen, in '51, '59, '62 and '63.

Tommy Schwall

Born: 1983

Olympic Year: 2002

Team: Ski Jumping

Schwall, who started jumping at age five, joined fellow Steamboat jumpers Clint Jones and Logan Gerber to take the J-II Junior Olympics team crown in Anchorage in 1999. Three years later, he and Jones reunited, this time with Alan Alborn and Brian Welch, to help the U.S. Jumping Team earn an 11th-place finish in the team K120 competition at the 2002 Olympics in Salt Lake. Schwall also competed for the U.S. at the World Juniors in 2000 and 2001 and took first at a 2002 Continental Cup competition.

Johnny Spillane

Born: 1980

Olympic Years: 1998, 2002

Team: Nordic Combined

Spillane came on strong in 2001, finishing as the top American (14th) in the sprint at the World Championships in Lahti, Finland. Though he did most of his training at Howelsen Hill before the team moved to Park City in 2002, Spillane, like the rest of the Olympic team members, was sponsored in part by the Steamboat Ski Corp., which earned them the nice perk of skiing for free on the slopes of Mount Werner. Like many Steamboat skiers—especially, for some reason, the Nordic guys—Johnny is a big fly-fishing fan who likes to hit the Yampa when the snow is gone.

John Steele

Born: 1909

Olympic Year: 1932

Team: Ski Jumping

Steamboat's first Olympian jumped at Lake Placid, but that was far from his first competition. Born in Minneapolis, Minnesota, Steele moved to Steamboat in 1918 and three years later, at the age of 12, took part in the jumping competition at the Steamboat Springs Winter Carnival. The winner, though it wasn't Steele, took home a 20-pound pail of lard. He didn't miss a Winter Carnival for the next 20 years. Steele skied with Carl Howelsen at Strawberry Park and made the most out of an early job shoveling snow off the bank roof at 8th and Lincoln. The way Steele figured it, the big pile of shoveled snow lent itself pretty well to building a jump, which he did. He and a friend jumped from the bank building until the sheriff made them quit because he was afraid they'd jump out in front of a passing car.

Tim Tetreault

Born: 1970

Olympic Years: 1992, 1994, 1998

Team: Nordic Combined

Tetreault earned three U.S. Nordic Combined titles, in '92, '93 and '97, before helping lead the team to a 10th-place finish at the Nagano Games in '98. He played soccer and tennis in high school in Vermont before moving to Steamboat in the summer of 1995. Like a lot of Yampa Valley skiers, Tetreault loves his golf, and he once joined a couple of Norwegians to play 126 holes in five days in San Diego.

Craig Thrasher

Born: 1970

Olympic Year: 1994

Team: Alpine

Thrasher competed in both slalom and downhill at the Lillehammer Olympics, finishing 31st in the downhill. A graduate of Steamboat Springs High School, Thrasher moved to Steamboat from Ohio with his parents in 1972. He finished first in the Rocky Mountain super G standings in 1989 and won FIS super G and downhill races the following year, at Sugarloaf and Jackson Hole, respectively. An excellent all-around athlete, Thrasher lettered for three years at Steamboat High in both football and track.

Carl Van Loan

Born: 1980

Olympic Year: 2002

Team: Nordic Combined

Van Loan, a road cycling competitor in high school, maintained his love for speed as a Nordic skier. He earned a berth on the 2000 World Cup team by skiing past 32 other racers to finish ninth in the sprint at the World Junior Championships. Van Loan skied in four World Junior Championships, and he helped the team earn a first-place finish in 1999 at Saalfelden, Austria.

Randy Weber

Born: 1977

Olympic Years: 1994, 1998

Team: Ski Jumping

Steamboat native Randy Webber set a hill record in Saint Petersburg, Russia, when he was 13 and was one of the most dominant juniors in the United States in 1992, winning both J-I and J-II 90-meter Junior Olympics competitions. Weber started skiing when he was three and jumping when he was six. He had three World Cup top 25 finishes during the '96 season, including a sixth at Predazzo, Italy.

Keith Wegeman

Born: 1929

Olympic Year: 1952

Teams: Nordic, Ski Jumping

A well-rounded athlete, Keith Wegeman was captain of the Steamboat Springs High School football team, worked summers as a lifeguard and used to write for *Sports Illustrated*. He attended the University of Denver, skiing for Willy Schaeffler's championship squads from 1949 to 1951. He won his first combined ski title at Winter Park in 1945 and was the highest finishing U.S. jumper at the Oslo Games, finishing in 12th place. The younger of two Olympian brothers, Wegeman went on to an acting career in Los Angeles, which included playing the Jolly Green Giant in a television commercial.

Paul Wegeman

Born: 1927

Olympic Year: 1952

Team: Nordic Combined

Paul Wegeman moved to Steamboat when he was 17 and performed well enough in high school to earn himself a scholarship to Western State College. However, like fellow jumper Marvin Crawford, Wegeman shortly found himself at the University of Denver, jumping for Willy Schaeffler. Wegeman worked as a ski patroller at Sun Valley, Idaho, in the 1940s, and also patrolled at Loveland, Winter Park and Berthoud, in Colorado. He was in 18th place in the Nordic Combined competition at the Oslo Olympics, but he suffered a bad fall and wasn't able to compete in the cross-country portion of the event.

Gladys "Skeeter" Werner

Born: 1933

Olympic Years: 1952, 1956

Team: Alpine

Skeeter was the first Werner Olympian, making the Olympic team that went to Cortina in 1956, where she finished in an impressive 10th place in the women's downhill. Buddy had won his first Hahnenkamm in 1954, and Skeeter and Buddy both made separate covers of *Sports Illustrated* the following year, as did Doak Walker, Heisman Trophy winner and Detroit Lions halfback, who Skeeter later married. In 1962 she became Steamboat's first ski school director, a position she held for eight years. Prior to that, Skeeter had been working in New York as a model and fashion consultant, but she returned home at the request of her brother, in part to help run the resort's first ski shop. Skeeter was inducted into the Colorado Ski Hall of Fame in 1984. She died in Steamboat in July 2001.

Loris "Bugs" Werner

Born: 1941

Olympic Years: 1964, 1968

Team: Alpine

The third of the Werner children to be coached by Gordy Wren, Loris said that much of his instruction came from Crosby Perry-Smith, who spent hours with him at Howelsen Hill. A strong downhiller like his brother, Loris won the U.S. National Downhill Championships in 1967, the eighth of his nine years on the U.S. Ski Team. After the '68 Olympics, he returned to Colorado and worked as the men's Junior National Team coach until joining his sister at the Steamboat ski school. He eventually worked his way up to mountain manager and vice president of operations. Loris says that the competition between him and his brother and sister played a big role in making them all better skiers. "Back then, everybody was thrown in together," he says. "There was no age differential, and nobody thought about it. You went out and played ball with whoever was there. I'd run against Buddy, I'd run against Skeeter, I'd run against whoever was in the gate next to me."

Wallace "Buddy" Werner

Born: 1936

Olympic Years: 1956, 1960, 1964

Team: Alpine

The influence that Buddy Werner has had on Steamboat Springs, both before and after his tragic death in 1964, cannot be summarized neatly in a few hundred words. Dozens of articles and at least one book—*I Never Look Back*, by John Rolfe Burroughs—have been written about the man who meant so much to this small town. Buddy came to represent much of what was good about the country in the 1950s, and he showed that Americans could beat the mighty Europeans at their own game. Nothing made that point stronger than his performances in two European downhills: the Hahnenkamm, in Austria, and the Holmemkollen, in Norway, where he was a three-time champion.

Buddy's parents, Hazie and Ed "Pop" Werner, went to watch him at the 1964 Olympics in Innsbruck. The children

Wallace "Buddy" Werner continued

had given them the trip for Christmas. After the Olympics, the whole family went to Winter Park, where Buddy competed in his last race before retiring. On April 2, 1964, he left for Austria to make a ski film for Willy Bogner. On the last day of filming, an enormous avalanche came down the mountain, burying Buddy and German ski star Barbi Henneberger. Hazie and Skeeter heard the news shortly after arriving at a ski show in Denver. Loris was told by a worker at a gas station. The news was hard on the entire town, which shortly thereafter renamed its library and its ski hill in his honor. Though he never won an Olympic medal, Buddy Werner will long be remembered as the man who brought pride to American skiing and made a small Colorado town extremely proud that he was one of their own.

Todd Wilson

Born: 1965
Olympic Years: 1988, 1992
Team: Nordic Combined

Todd Wilson moved from Winter Park to Steamboat so he could attend Colorado Mountain College and train with the Steamboat Springs Winter Sports Club. He was already a nine-year veteran of the U.S. Ski Team when he made it to his second Olympics, in Albertville, France, in 1992. Though he always had strong North American performances, Wilson was never able to break into the top 20 in World Cup Nordic competition. He returned to Steamboat in 1995 to become a jump coach at Howelsen Hill.

Gordy Wren

Born: 1919
Olympic Year: 1948
Teams: Alpine, Ski Jumping, Nordic Combined, Nordic

Gordy Wren remains the only American skier to qualify for all four ski disciplines—alpine, cross-country, jumping and Nordic Combined—in the same Olympics. "I was running into myself over there," he said of his 1948 experience in St. Moritz. As a junior, Wren competed in 75 jumping competitions and won 72 of them. After retiring from competition he became a coach with the Steamboat Springs Winter Sports Club, building the jumping program up from four skiers to 32 in only two years. In addition to managing the Howelsen Hill and Mount Werner ski areas in Steamboat, Wren coached, taught or managed at Alta, Utah; Winter Park, Colorado; the University of Denver; Jackson Hole, Wyoming; Loveland Basin, Colorado; and Reno, Nevada. He was also an instructor with the Army's 10th Mountain Division. Wren was inducted into the National Ski Hall of Fame in 1958.

Bibliography

Books

A History of Skiing in Colorado, by Abbott Fay, 2000

Dancers on Horseback, The Perry-Mansfield Story, by Lucile Bogue, 1984

Diary of Lulie Margie Crawford, A Little Girl's View of the Old West, 1880-1881

Headfirst in the Pickel Barrel, by John Rolfe Burroughs, 1963

Historic Hahns Peak, by Thelma V. Stevenson, 1976

John Daniel Crawford in the Great Good Old Days, by Lulita Crawford Pritchett, 1984

Legends, A Centennial Collection, by Deb Olsen, 1999

Maggie by My Side, by Lulita Crawford Pritchett, 1983

Miracle on a Mountain, by Lucile Bogue, 1985

My First Eighty One Years, by R. Wayne Light, 1984

The Flying Norseman, by Leif Hovelsen, 1983

Remember the Old Yampa Valley, by Lulita Crawford Pritchett, 1983

The Cabin at Medicine Springs, by Lulita Crawford Pritchett, 1958

The History of Skiing at Steamboat Springs, by Sureva Towler, 1987

The Sand Creek Massacre, by Stan Hoig, 1961

Steamboat Springs and the "Treacherous and Speedy Skee" by Jean Wren, 1978

Shepherdess of Elk River Valley, by Margaret Duncan Brown, 1967

Ski Racing Redbook, 1973, 1974, 1975, 1976

Steamboat Round the Bend, by Dee Richards, 1976

Steamboat Springs, the First 40 Years, by Lee Powell, 1972

Articles

"A Century of Stores" supplement to the *Steamboat Pilot*, August 16, 2000

"A Circle of Magic, Perry Mansfield Camp Fulfills A Dream," by Toni Lanza, *Steamboat* Magazine, Summer/Fall 1981

"A Lift into the Jet Age," by Keith Kramer, *Steamboat* Magazine, Winter/Spring 1987

"A Memory of Bud Werner," by Bob Beattie *SKIING* Magazine, October, 1964

"Dance Camp Saved in Last-minute Deal," Deborah Ward, *The Steamboat Pilot*, September 9, 1993

"From Little Toot to the Olympics," by Christine McKelvie, *Steamboat* Magazine, Winter, 1980

"From the Werners to the World Cup," by Mike Clark, *Steamboat* Magazine, Winter/Spring, 1990

"F.M. Light & Sons—Granddaddy of Local Merchants," by Nancy Ellis, *Steamboat* Magazine, Winter/Spring 1993

"Hazie Werner, Grand Lady of the Valley," by Rod Hanna, *Steamboat Springs* Magazine, Winter, 1980

"Howelsen Hill: Steamboat's Remarkable Jumping Complex," by Dave Thiemann, *Steamboat* Magazine, Winter/Spring 1982

"John Fetcher, Modern Pioneer," *Steamboat* Magazine, Winter 1985

"Lake Catamount, A Genesis," by Rod Hanna, *Steamboat* Magazine, Winter, 1986

"Mountain Towns of North America: Steamboat Springs," by Abby Rand, *SKI* Magazine, October, 1973

"Our Cool College," by George Bagwell, *Steamboat Visitor's Guide,* Winter/Spring, 1988

"The First Winter Special Olympics Remembered," *Steamboat Springs* Magazine, Winter 1978

"The Flat Tops—Birthplace of the American Wilderness Movement," by Keith Kramer, *Steamboat* Magazine, Summer, 1987.

"The Great Western Freestyle Center," *Steamboat Springs* Magazine, Winter, 1981

"The Making of a Modern Resort," by Pete Wither, *Steamboat* Magazine, Summer/Fall 1985

"The Man Behind the Kidd," by Rod Hanna, *Steamboat* Magazine, Winter/Spring 1984

"The Miracle of Steamboat," *SKI* Magazine, December, 1956

"The Namesake of Rudi's Run," by Tom Ross, *Steamboat* Magazine, Winter/Spring 1986

The Shady Side of the River," by Jean Wren, *Steamboat* Magazine, Summer/Fall, 1984

"The Tugboat River Race—A Steamboat Tradition," *Steamboat* Magazine, Summer, 1979

"Skeeter, Crown Princess of the Noble House of Werner." *Steamboat* Magazine, Winter/Spring 1986

"Sven Wiik, Guru of American Cross Country Skiing," by David Sumner *Steamboat* Magazine, Winter/Spring 1986

"Wee Gordy, Big Mountain," *SKIING* Magazine, 1968

"Where Do We Go from Here?" *Steamboat Springs* Magazine, Winter/Spring 1983

Interviews

John Fetcher, March 15, Steamboat Springs, Colorado

Mike Diener March 16, Steamboat

Pete Wither, April 1, Steamboat

Ed and Jayne Hill. April 13, Steamboat

Nelson Carmichael, via e-mail, from Hood River, Oregon

Vernon Summer, May 5, Steamboat

Jean Wren, May 5, Steamboat

Lloyd and Annabeth Lockhart, May 25, Steamboat

Jim and Audrey Temple, June 4, Boulder, Colorado

Marvin Crawford, June 7, Denver, Colorado

Loris and Deb Werner June 15, Steamboat

Hans Geier, June 16, Steamboat

Park Smalley, June 23, via telephone, from Spokane, Washington

Jon Smalley, June 23, via telephone, from Steamboat

Merle Nash, July 13, Steamboat

Irene Nelsen, July 14, Steamboat

Moose Barrows, July 20, Steamboat

Rod Hanna, July 21, Steamboat

Hank Edwards and Larry Lamb July 21, Steamboat

David Wren, July 22, via telephone, from Steamboat

Charles Leckenby, August 3, via telephone, from Steamboat

Mix Beavais, August 10, Steamboat

Steve Elkins, August 11, Steamboat

Hank Perry, August 26, Steamboat

Billy Kidd, September 14, Boulder, Colorado

John Wisch, September 15, via telephone, from Hood River, Oregon

Glen Paulk, September 17, via telephone, from Steamboat

Hank Kashiwa, September 18, via telephone, from Florida

Martin Hart, September 18, Denver, Colorado

Ray Heid, September 19, via telephone, from Steamboat

Dan Gilchrist, September 20, Steamboat

Kent Ericksen, September 22, Steamboat

Tom Wood, October 9, via telephone, from Steamboat

Lance Romick, October 16, via telephone, from Steamboat

Sherman Poppen, October 23, via telephone, from Steamboat

Charlie Meyers, October 38, via telephone, from Denver

Paul Wegeman, November 3, Colorado Springs, Colorado

Ben Tiffany, November 5, via telephone, from Steamboat

Shannon Dunn, November 8, via telephone, from San Diego

Photographers

Aryeh Copa

Ron Dahlquist

Dan Gilchrist

Tim Hancock

Rod Hanna

Cynthia Hunter

Corey Kopischke

Chris Patterson

Larry Pierce

Tom Ross

Smokey Vandergrift

Acknowledgments

First I'd like to thank the entire Mountain Sports Press staff—Bill Grout, Chris Salt, Michelle Schrantz, Scott Kronberg, Megan Selkey, Alan Stark and Andy Hawk—for their tireless efforts in completing this project. Also thanks to Perkins Miller, Helen Olsson, Evelyn Spence and the rest of the staff at *Skiing* Magazine for putting up with me while my candle burned at both ends.

I have many people to thank in Steamboat: Andy Wirth, Mike Lane, Cathy Wiedemer Billy Kidd, Larry Pierce and Riley Polumbus at the Steamboat Ski and Resort Corporation; Marty Woodbury and Candice Lombardo at the Tread of Pioneers Museum; Mary Zeigler of the Winter Sports Club; Jennifer Bartlett, who helped immensely with photo research; the entire staff at Paddler magazine, especially Eugene Buchanan and Jim Marsh, who provided tables to write on and couches to sleep on; Alysa Selby and the rest of the staff at Bud Werner Memorial Library; Tom Ross, Deb Olsen, Eugene Buchanan and Sureva Towler, whose well-written sidebars added immeasurably to the book; to everyone at the Steamboat Pilot, who helped me track down photos, to Mike and Kathy Deimer for great breakfasts at Johnny B Goods; and to each and every person who graciously took the time to let me interview them (see list below).

Also, thanks the entire Temple family for their research assistance; to David Gonzales for inspiration; to Eric Paddack of the Colorado Historical Society and Joe Kelley of the Grand County Historical Society; to Jayne Hill and Vernon Summer, who helped proofread the historical chapters; to Keely Payton and April Darrow for drinks; to Jamie Gormley for distractions; and to all the photographers who sent me their spectacular work, especially Aryeh Copa , who shot on demand when I found holes that needed to be filled.

Index

Index

Photo Credits